# DEVIL'S ADVOCATES

**DEVIL'S ADVOCATES** is a series of books devoted to exploring the classics of horror cinema. Contributors to the series come from the fields of teaching, academia, journalism and fiction, but all have one thing in common: a passion for the horror film and a desire to share it with the widest possible audience.

'The admirable Devil's Advocates series is not only essential – and fun – reading for the serious horror fan but should be set texts on any genre course.'
**Dr Ian Hunter, Reader in Film Studies, De Montfort University, Leicester**

'Auteur Publishing's new Devil's Advocates critiques on individual titles... offer bracingly fresh perspectives from passionate writers. The series will perfectly complement the BFI archive volumes.' **Christopher Fowler,** *Independent on Sunday*

'Devil's Advocates has proven itself more than capable of producing impassioned, intelligent analyses of genre cinema... quickly becoming the go-to guys for intelligent, easily digestible film criticism.' ***Horror Talk.com***

'Auteur Publishing continue the good work of giving serious critical attention to significant horror films.' ***Black Static***

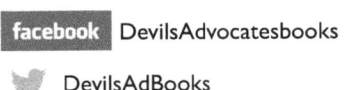 DevilsAdvocatesbooks

DevilsAdBooks

**ALSO AVAILABLE IN THIS SERIES**

*Antichrist* Amy Simmons

*Black Sunday* Martyn Conterio

*The Blair Witch Project* Peter Turner

*Candyman* Jon Towlson

*Cannibal Holocaust* Calum Waddell

*Carrie* Neil Mitchell

*The Company of Wolves* James Gracey

*Creepshow* Simon Brown

*The Curse of Frankenstein* Marcus K. Harmes

*Dead of Night* Jez Conolly & David Bates

*The Descent* James Marriot

*The Devils* Darren Arnold

*Don't Look Now* Jessica Gildersleeve

*The Fly* Emma Westwood

*Frenzy* Ian Cooper

*Halloween* Murray Leeder

*House of Usher* Evert Jan van Leeuwen

*In the Mouth of Madness* Michael Blyth

*It Follows* Joshua Grimm

*Ju-on The Grudge* Marisa Hayes

*Let the Right One In* Anne Billson

*Macbeth* Rebekah Owens

*Nosferatu* Cristina Massaccesi

*Saw* Benjamin Poole

*Scream* Steven West

*The Shining* Laura Mee

*The Silence of the Lambs* Barry Forshaw

*Suspiria* Alexandra Heller-Nicholas

*The Texas Chain Saw Massacre* James Rose

*The Thing* Jez Conolly

*Twin Peaks: Fire Walk With Me* Lindsay Hallam

*Witchfinder General* Ian Cooper

**FORTHCOMING**

*Blood and Black Lace* Roberto Curti

*Daughters of Darkness* Kat Ellinger

*The Mummy* Doris V. Sutherland

*Shivers* Luke Aspell

# Devil's Advocates

# M

# Samm Deighan

First published in 2019 by
Auteur, 24 Hartwell Crescent, Leighton Buzzard LU7 1NP
www.auteur.co.uk
Copyright © Auteur 2019

Series design: Nikki Hamlett at Cassels Design
Set by Cassels Design www.casselsdesign.co.uk

All rights reserved. No part of this publication may be reproduced in any material form (including photocopying or storing in any medium by electronic means and whether or not transiently or incidentally to some other use of this publication) without the permission of the copyright owner.

British Library Cataloguing-in-Publication Data
A catalogue record for this book is available from the British Library

ISBN paperback: 978-1-911325-77-2
ISBN ebook: 978-1-911325-78-9

# Contents

Introduction: Fire, Voices and Torment ..................................................................... 7

Chapter One: A Murderer Among Us ..................................................................... 15

Chapter Two: In the Hall of the Mountain King ..................................................... 33

Chapter Three: The Vampire of Düsseldorf and the Butcher of Hanover ............ 51

Chapter Four: While the City Sleeps ....................................................................... 69

Chapter Five: The Pleasure to End All Pleasures .................................................... 89

Bibliography ............................................................................................................. 104

# Introduction: Fire, Voices and Torment

Fritz Lang's seminal *M* (1931) exists in a liminal space between social drama, crime thriller and horror film, but belongs in a larger discussion of horror genre cinema because of its widespread influence: with this film, Lang effectively created the serial killer movie. *M* follows the paedophiliac killer Hans Beckert (Peter Lorre), who is pursued by local police, distraught parents and the criminal underworld for his horrifying and compulsive murders of Berlin's children. Exploring the themes of systemic violence, mob justice and urban paranoia, *M* presents an evolution of the subject matter found in Lang's earlier crime films, like *Dr. Mabuse der Spieler / Dr. Mabuse the Gambler* (1922) and *Spione / Spies* (1928), with a focus on abnormal psychology as a source of terrifying monstrosity. The film is also rich in historical detail, lending itself to discussions of political, sociological and psychological significance. The aim of this book is to situate *M* not only within the developing body of twentieth-century horror films, but as a progenitor of genre cinema, as the origin point of a filmic thread that includes Hitchcock's *Shadow of a Doubt* (1943) and *Psycho* (1960), Michael Powell's *Peeping Tom* (1960) and Michael Mann's *Manhunter* (1986), among others.

Peter Hogue writes that *M* is Lang's 'greatest accomplishment and the pivotal film of his career,'[1] a sentiment with which Lang certainly agreed; he voiced repeatedly over the years that he thought it was his best work. Hogue writes: 'Lang's great accomplishment (in *M* above all) is to have dramatized both the alienation of modern social reality and the abiding interrelatedness of human beings in even the most unresolved of modern dilemmas.'[2] Lang achieves this by blending elements of the horror film with a realist social drama; he compares and contrasts working class families in the city with a serial killer, child-victims, underworld criminals, cops and the teeming mass of the city. *M* explores some of Lang's recurring concerns about law and order, in the sense that order is largely dispensed by an underground criminal network and by mob justice in a kangaroo court.

In terms of how *M* presents hysteria and paranoia in urban society, the film is also a chilling glimpse into pre-WWII German society. Dana Stevens writes,

The letter M, in the form of a title, marks a crucial point in the history of German cinema as well as in the career of Fritz Lang. It is Lang's first sound film, it appears one year before the assumption to power of the Nazi party, and it is the last German film of Lang's actually to be seen in Germany (the only subsequent one, 1933's *Testament of Dr. Mabuse*, would be banned before it even came out).[3]

*M* depicts a Berlin on the verge of totalitarian control. The police raids, media frenzy and government surveillance are a result of Beckert's horrible child killings, though this exertion of state power is ineffectual. Berlin's citizens are forced to team up with the criminal underworld to protect their children. Peter Hogue writes, 'In *M*, the shifting, "multiple" point of view produces a sense of an intricately tangled human bond. We variously share the perspectives of cop, petty criminal, murderer, victims, perpetrators and a menagerie of stray urban souls.'[4] *M* is ultimately a film about the danger of succumbing to mass hysteria, a theme Lang would return to many times throughout his career.

Born in fin de siècle Vienna as Friedrich Christian Anton Lang, Fritz Lang travelled the world, studied painting in Paris, and served in WWI before beginning a career in cinema that would permanently alter the medium. Soon after the war, he found a job at Germany's most prestigious studio, Universum Film AG (generally known as Ufa), where he began writing and directing films. Many of his silent productions in the 1920s were collaborations with his then wife, script writer and novelist Thea von Harbou, and the couple frequently explored issues of paranoia, surveillance, social control and mob justice—making his films increasingly unpopular with the Nazis as they rose to power in the late '20s and early '30s.

Lang draws a disturbing parallel between cops and criminals in *M*; both are shown plotting in dark, grimy rooms choked with cigar smoke, and there is no real distinction made between the law and lawlessness. The men portrayed throughout the film are not likable, fleshed out characters, but grotesque silhouettes. On the surface, this is a film about a community seeking vigilante justice against a child killer. But on closer reflection, the motivations for justice are shallow and even selfish. The criminals want Beckert off the street so that business can go on as usual, while the police similarly want a return to the status quo. Lang's film is a scathing indictment of the culture he was soon to flee from and a country that was on the verge of dramatic, unthinkable change.

A sense of horror within the film is rooted in the fact that there is no clear hero or villain. Unlike *Dr. Mabuse the Gambler*, Beckert is no evil mastermind, but a man who is shown to be increasingly lonely and tormented. *M*'s success as a horror film comes from the fact that Lang encourages us to sympathise with Beckert. This is possible thanks to a mesmerizing, very physical performance from Peter Lorre, a talented Austro-Hungarian stage actor who became a star because of *M*. His Beckert is at once pathetic, sick, mad, manipulative and desperate. Lang and cinematographer Fritz Arno Wagner shot him through frames, windows and in mirror reflections, symbolic of his fragmented psyche and growing madness. Though his acts are horrific, his assertion that he has no control over himself and is possessed by some terrible force is chilling. He ultimately seems like a victim as he screams, 'I have no control over this, this evil thing inside of me! The fire, the voices, the torment!'

Hans Beckert (Peter Lorre) contemplates the horror of his crimes in *M*.

## FILM SYNOPSIS

*M* opens with children in the courtyard of an apartment tenement singing a nursery rhyme about a man in black who will chop you up. The tenement is also populated with mothers—in the process of doing laundry and other mundane household chores—one of whom stops the children from singing, because the song reminds her of real murders. It's revealed, through a wanted poster plastered on the side of a building offering a reward for 10,000 Deutsche Marks, that a child murderer is at large in Berlin. Later that afternoon, little Elsie Beckmann (child actress Inge Landgut, who would appear later that year in Gerhard Lamprecht's *Emil und die Detektive / Emil and the Detectives* (1931)), is interrupted while bouncing a ball on her return home from school by the harmless-looking Hans Beckert, who is tunelessly whistling a bar from Edvard Grieg's 'In the Hall of the Mountain King'. Beckert buys Elsie a doll-shaped balloon from a blind street vendor (regular Lang collaborator Georg John) and leads her away.

Elsie's mother (Ellen Widmann), who is preparing lunch at home, notices her daughter is late to arrive and begins to panic when the doorbell rings and it's a magazine salesman instead of Elsie. This scene culminates in shots of Elsie's ball rolling on its own through the grass and her balloon being caught in some telephone wires before it blows away: without showing us her corpse, Lang makes it clear that Elsie Beckmann has been murdered.

This is later confirmed by paperboys announcing the news on the street and selling papers to a gathering, increasingly panicked crowd, who discuss that there have been eight murders so far. Beckert, meanwhile, writes a letter to the newspapers—his first to the police has apparently been ignored—to let them know that he will kill again. Over the next few days, newspapers encourage mothers to be vigilant, while the police are clearly at a loss thanks to the lack of clues and the public is in a state of near panic. An inspector admits, 'Any man in the street could be the guilty one'. An older man is almost the victim of mob violence, when a child stops him on the street to ask for the time. The man is regarded suspiciously and is nearly attacked. A crowd gangs up on him, declaring that he's the murderer. They demand action from two passing policemen.

Police use the latest technology, including fingerprinting, to try to extract evidence from Beckert's letters. Though they are unable to get any usable prints, experts note that the handwriting indicates 'strong and pathological sexuality'. Inspector Lohmann (Otto Wernicke, who would appear in Lang's 1933 film *Das Testament des Dr. Mabuse / The Testament of Dr. Mabuse*) is pressured by government officials to find the killer by whatever means necessary. His men speak to witnesses, examine clues left in the park where Elsie was murdered, and have begun to harass flop houses, homeless people and bars throughout the city.

Lohmann admits that this intrusion makes people nervous, emphasised by eerie, expressionistic sequences of individuals walking alone in the city at night, clearly avoiding one another and sticking to the shadows. There is a hint of martial law, as black-clad police officers raid random streets, roughing people up and carting them off without any apparent cause. An entire bar is rounded up and forced to show their papers, and many are arrested. Bar owners—and the criminal underworld in general—are increasingly enraged that their business is disrupted night after night.

The city's criminals discuss that 'there are more police on the street tonight than whores'. These men—representing various factions of the criminal underworld—resolve that they must find and put a stop to the child murderer because he's ruining their business, under the guidance of Der Schränker ('The Safecracker', played by Gustaf Gründgens; he would later find fame and notoriety for giving one of the greatest performances of the titular character of *Faust* on stage, but also for alleged collaboration with the Nazis).

The police, meanwhile, have become desperate. They are sure that the killer is 'a man who looks like he wouldn't hurt a fly', and discuss possible ways to catch him, such as offering a reward or hiring a psychic. Anticipating modern cinematic depictions of serial killers, Lang stresses that 'the criminal and the victim are connected only by chance; an instantaneous impulse is the killer's only motive'. He draws a clear parallel between the cops and criminals by cutting back and forth between the two groups as they sit around tables, smoke cigarettes, pace in small rooms, and try to figure out inspired ways to catch Beckert. The underworld decides that they will harness the beggars' union to follow and watch the children; Berlin is mapped out and they're all assigned blocks.

Beckert narrowly avoids being questioned by the police, who come to his flat when he happens to be away, attempting to prey on another child. After some anxious waiting and a failed attempt, he finds a little girl on her own. He buys her a balloon from the same blind street vendor, who recognises Beckert's whistle and convinces a young man on the street to follow Beckert. Beckert leads the girl down a deserted street and to a bakery, where he buys her some sweets. The boy stays close on their trail and writes 'M'—for Mörder (meaning murderer)—in chalk on his palm; he discreetly pretends to run into Beckert, leaving the 'M' on the back of Beckert's coat. Though the little girl tells him about the chalk on his coat and he tries to wipe it away, he's already been spotted; this puts the beggars and ultimately the entire underworld on his trail.

Beckert runs into a building full of empty offices, as the criminals corner him. He hides in the basement, in a crowded storage room, and is accidentally locked in by a security guard. The criminals, meanwhile, decide not to turn him over to the police, but to deal with him themselves once he has been captured. They infiltrate the building and pursue him to the attic. He nearly escapes and the watchman—who the criminals have tied up—sets off the alarm, alerting the police, but they finally manage to corner him. They make a mass exodus from the building and carry him out, tied up in a bag. He is led to an underground kangaroo court in what looks like the basement of an abandoned warehouse, which is packed with members of the community, including many mothers. They admit that they will try him for his crimes and kill him. Terrified, he admits that he's driven to kill and the urge is always following him. He says he's haunted by ghosts—of the children he's killed and their mothers—and these spectres only stop tormenting him when he kills. He is spared from violent death, at the last moment, by police who raid the warehouse and whisk Beckert off to be tried in a criminal court, depriving the mothers of their vengeance.

## *M*: AN ANALYSIS

Thanks to its complexity, *M* can be discussed as a horror film, an influential serial killer thriller, a portrait of city life, and a historical, political document. In Chapter One, I will establish the context for the climate in which *M* was produced, as well as its historical context within early '30s Germany during the rise of Nazism. The film will be explored in connection to Lang's early work, during a period when he experimented with genre the most radically, including romance, science fiction, fantasy and crime thrillers. I will discuss how *M* marks a turning point in Lang's career, when he began to fixate overwhelmingly on characters in the grip of social paranoia; after *M*, he almost exclusively made crime films and thrillers with similar themes. The discussion will also include *M*'s relationship to the German expressionist cinema of the '10s and '20s, particularly those films that fit within the horror genre, such as *Der Student von Prag / The Student of Prague* (1913), *Das Cabinet des Dr. Caligari / The Cabinet of Dr. Caligari* (1920) and *Nosferatu, eine Symphonie des Grauens / Nosferatu: A Symphony of Horror* (1922), many of which similarly focused on themes of madness and violence.

Chapter Two will explore one of the themes that I believe positions *M* as an important entry in early horror cinema: its use of the murderer as protagonist. Though Hitchcock began to tread similar ground with *The Lodger* (1927), the films are radically different in the protagonists they focus on—for example, Hitchcock keeps the identity of his killer a mystery, while Lang reveals his immediately—and the way they portray violence. Additionally, I will explore how star Peter Lorre's portrayal of Beckert not only shaped his career, but went on to influence future sympathetic serial killer characters.

Chapter Three will explore the numerous ways in which *M* prefigured and captured our growing understanding of serial murder, and particularly its expression in cinema. Unusually for the time, Lang used a number of true crime sources and his intensive research required him to spend several days in a mental asylum; he was inspired by several real-life German child killers—like Fritz Haarmann, Peter Kürten and Carl Großmann—several of whom he allegedly interviewed. This chapter compares and contrasts *M* and Lang's work during the period with other German films that portray violent killers as their protagonists, such as those made by F.W. Murnau and G.W. Pabst; not only in terms of how these protagonists are portrayed, but how their respective directors deal with the intersection of violence, death and sexuality.

Chapter Four explores how Lang suggests in *M* that the city itself, particularly the city as a product of modernity, is somehow responsible for madness, moral evil and the existence of a monster like Beckert. Further, I will explore how the film is also about a community in the grip of fear and paranoia in a way that subverts a more straightforward social drama—such as the Weimar street film, popular at the time *M* was made—because Lang's kangaroo court represents a divided social strata essentially united only by violence. This suggests that the kind of violence enacted by Beckert is not the exception but the rule; it is not only the product of a diseased mind, but is something anyone could be capable of. Additionally, I will use this chapter to explore the film's production, namely how Lang made use of the city of Berlin itself in a sort of proto-neorealist sense, down to employing non-professional actors from among the city's criminal class.

The book will conclude with an examination of *M*'s legacy and how Lang's portrayal of a serial killer as protagonist went on to influence subsequent horror films and serial killer thrillers. In place of the supernatural or mad science, as was popular with horror cinema in the '30s, '40s and '50s, Lang innovatively used abnormal psychology as a source of monstrosity. In this way, it influenced everything from the emerging serial killer thriller subgenre to film noir through titles like *Stranger on the Third Floor* (1940), *Hangover Square* (1945), Lang's own *Secret Beyond the Door* (1947) and *In a Lonely Place* (1959). I will also discuss how Lang continued to explore *M*'s themes in his own later films and how they influenced more contemporary depictions of serial killers in both arthouse cinema and mainstream horror films like *The Silence of the Lambs* (1991) or *Se7en* (1995), giving an overview of how *M* has influenced contemporary genre cinema and changing depictions of serial killers on film.

**FOOTNOTES**

1. Peter Hogue, 'Fritz Lang: Our Contemporary,' Film Comment, Vol. 26, No. 6 (November-December 1990), p. 10.
2. Ibid., p. 12.
3. Dana Stevens, 'Writing, Scratching, and Politics from M to Mabuse,' Qui Parle, Vol. 7, No. 1, Nation and Fantasy (Fall/Winter 1993), p. 69.
4. Peter Hogue (1990), p. 12.

# Chapter One: A Murderer Among Us

> The weird pleasure the Germans take in evoking horror can perhaps be ascribed to the excessive and very Germanic desire to submit to discipline, together with a certain proneness to sadism. — Lotte Eisner, *The Haunted Screen*

*M* can be read as a depiction of modernity as monstrosity. The city features as a character in and of itself—often dwarfing Peter Lorre's Hans Beckert until he seems a tiny and pathetic figure—but it is not just any urban domain; Lang specifically portrays Berlin, the seat of both German culture and government, as it was in 1930-1931. The city is crucial to the events of the film: it begins with working class children in the courtyard of a tenement, where they are carefully watched over by paranoid mothers. The children sing their eerie nursery rhyme about the man in black, and Lang immediately establishes that in such a crowded terrain, they are easily victimised. Indeed, within moments, Beckert has targeted and begun to stalk young Elsie Beckmann on her way home from school. She becomes his prey with minimal effort when he buys her a balloon and leads her into an expansive park—Berlin is known for its numerous parks—where there is presumably enough privacy for him to carry out her murder undetected, and mercifully off-screen. To indicate what is happening, Lang includes a shot of the ball she was bouncing, as it rolls away on its own through some grass, and her balloon—disturbingly in a primitive doll-like shape—caught in some telephone wires before it floats up into the sky, out of view.

The city also serves as a source of exposition. Within the film's first few moments, Beckert's crimes are revealed to the audience via urban media: newspapers, magazines, wanted posters and word of mouth on the streets. Outside of Beckert himself, Lang portrays the film's characters not as individual protagonists or supporting figures, but as a sort of chaotic Greek chorus split between grieving mothers, the Berlin underworld and frustrated police officers and government officials. There is the implication that the police have had trouble locating Beckert and narrowing down the killer's identity, because theoretically anyone could be responsible for the crimes. Suspects crowd the horizon, while every piece of detritus is a potential clue, evoking Lang's earlier films *Dr. Mabuse the Gambler* and *Metropolis* (1927), where the city is a cesspool of paranoia, corruption and human evil. In *M*, there is the implication that Beckert is a product of this city; not a monstrous anomaly, but an inevitable consequence of urban civilisation.

The bustling crowd before a 'wanted' poster in *M*.

While some later serial killer films cover a wide range of territory, involve a travelling protagonist, and hover around rural spaces, such as *Psycho* and *The Silence of the Lambs*, this focus on the city as a hotbed for psychosexual crime would reappear in later serial killer-themed films after *M* and is one of its central features to which I will return. As with Lang's Berlin, many of these later films captured a particular time and place, such as San Francisco in the '70s in Don Siegel's *Dirty Harry* (1971), London in the '70s in Hitchcock's *Frenzy* (1972), or New York in the '80s in Mary Harron's *American Psycho* (2000). In this sense, it's difficult not to read *M* as a chilling postcard from a society on the brink, about to plunge into a over a decade of fascism, total war and industrialised violence.

*M* was made during the last bitter months of the so-called Weimar Republic, named for the German city where its first constitutional assembly was held in August of 1919, though Berlin was the government's capital city. Though known as the Deutsches Reich or Deutsches Republik during its fourteen-year run and not referred to as the Weimar Republic until later in the '30s, this government quickly became associated with what the Nazis later perceived to be its faults: abject poverty, inflation and corruption, sexual debauchery and chaos in the streets. While it is undeniable that the country suffered a major depression during this period—one that ended in early 1933 when Hitler assumed the chancellorship—the November Revolution of 1918-1919 brought with it previously unknown political and personal freedom as the German state struggled to reinvent itself and establish a new political identity.

Many of the Weimar Republic's troubles, as reflected in M, relate to the fact that the '20s were a period of profound flux for the country. In the late '10s, Germany reeled from the aftershock of World War I, the sudden upheaval of deeply entrenched imperialism, and the perceived tragedy of the Treaty of Versailles, which required Germany to make extensive war reparations. A particularly glaring issue was the nation's inability to bridge the violent, growing maw between left and right-wing extremists that found its way from the streets into Germany's government. The massive Reichswehr, or imperial army, had been disbanded after WWI with little by way of compensation for many former soldiers—generally angry young men—who often joined paramilitary groups such as the various right-wing Freikorps factions and their later offshoots by default, because the newly formed army was too small to accommodate many of them by mandate of the Treaty of Versailles.

It is this atmosphere of imminent violence and urban chaos that Lang captures in M, where mob rule takes the place of law and order and the city's criminal network is ubiquitous. Lang's M does not depict the infamous bloody battles between communists and fascists of the early '20s, the social changes in favour of workers, or the golden age of art and culture in the country, but instead evokes a world of hyperinflation, where the stereotypical wheelbarrow full of marks was barely enough to buy a loaf of bread and both left and right factions blamed the Republic and bitterly mistrusted their own government. M—and the Berlin it depicts—mirrors the world found in something like George Grosz's painting 'Berlin Street' (1931), a crowded grey and brown landscaped packed with furtive, grotesque figures. The Metropolitan Museum of Art catalogue describes it as, 'the modern metropolis, a hellish place animated by greed, cruelty, and ghoulish lust. [...] Distorted, soulless automatons, the figures appear as slaves to capitalistic decadence'.[5]

In reality, by 1929 the economy had begun to stabilise and the Dawes Plan—a new arrangement that made the country dependent on American banks—essentially allowed Germany to skirt the reparations demanded by the Treaty of Versailles. But these positive changes were fleeting, partly thanks to the Wall Street Crash of 1929, which plunged Germany into a related depression. Nationally, this was perceived as a failure of the Republic, and in particular the Social Democrats, who had been predominantly in power under Chancellor Hermann Müller. He was forced to resign in early 1930, when the situation seemed particularly grim. In response, right wing forces crept in and by January of 1930, the National Socialists acquired their first substantial seat of political power when Wilhelm Frick became Minister of the Interior of the state of Thuringia. Not long after, the Nazis became the second biggest political party in the country, coinciding with the removal of French troops—a peacekeeping force per the Treaty of Versailles—from the Rhineland.

Historian William L. Shirer argues that Adolf Hitler was convinced the economy would take a sharp downturn and was biding his time for such a moment.

> The years from 1925 until the coming of the depression in 1929 were lean years for Adolf Hitler and the Nazi movement. [...] Despite the excitability of his nature, which often led to outbursts of hysteria, he had the patience to wait and the shrewdness to realize that the climate of material prosperity and a feeling of relaxation which settled over Germany in those years was not propitious for his purposes. He was confident that the good times would not last.[6]

These years of prosperity and 'relaxation' that defined the so-called Roaring Twenties (or Golden Twenties as they were known in Germany) led to a nation unprepared for such hardship, particularly considering the fact that Germany had just really begun to recover from their failure in WWI. Unemployment was widespread, banks and small businesses closed, and international trade ceased, wreaking havoc on not just the German market, but all of Europe. Shirer writes,

> Without exports, German industry could not keep its plants going, and production fell by almost half from 1929 to 1932. Millions were thrown out of work. [...] The whole Western world was stricken by forces which its leaders did not understand and which they felt were beyond man's control. How was it possible that suddenly there could be so much poverty, so much human suffering, in the midst of so much plenty?[7]

While Lang does not overtly address this economic depression and political chaos within *M*'s dialogue, these themes are ever present in the film's depictions of urban strife, mob justice, and the extensive criminal network in the Berlin underground, who prove to be more effective at dispensing law and order than the police force. There is tension on the streets and violence seems ever imminent. This is hinted at in an early scene, when a well-dressed elderly man briefly assisting a child on the street is considered a suspect by hysterical passers-by who corner him with increasing aggression and flag down a policeman. The incident is instigated by an enormous, brutish man who could easily be taken by contemporary audiences for one of the *Sturmabteilung* or SA, the Nazi Party's unruly paramilitary arm, who would soon be replaced by the more organised, ruthless *Schutzstaffel* or SS in 1934.

Thanks to the SA's reputation as thugs, the Nazi Party gained a degree of legitimacy and respectability when they publicly ousted the SA during what is known as the Night of the Long Knives in 1934, leading to hundreds arrested or murdered. But this process of legitimisation began with the Depression, as desperate citizens turned in greater numbers to the more radical political parties on the left (the communists) or the right (the fascists). And because many perceived the left-leaning Social Democrats to be responsible for the failures of the Republic, an alarming number of voters began to reconsider the potential effectiveness of the Nazis, resulting in the breakdown of the parliamentary system of the Reichstag and yet another haphazard reformation of the German Republic.

A parallel can be drawn between *M* and real-life events, in the sense that Lang turns Beckert's crimes into an excuse for introducing what is essentially martial law across the city. The police commit raids at will, demonstrated in a particularly lengthy sequence in the first act of the film. A commissioner uses seemingly any excuse to send a number of bar patrons to city headquarters, whether they have their identity papers on them or not. Their belongings are confiscated and, in a chilling sequence captured in a tracking shot, are shown to be organised on a long table by type: weapons, wallets and other miscellanea. It is difficult for a contemporary viewer not to associate this with the Nazi hoarding of their concentration camp victims' possessions, which they would sort in different rooms, by type: suitcases, clothing, gold teeth and jewellry and human hair; human lives reduced to categorised piles of personal objects.

An event that would occur not long after the release of *M*, Hitler's passing of the Enabling Act of 1933, is considered the official end of the Weimar Republic by many historians, allowing as it did Hitler, the newly named chancellor, and his cabinet to bypass any legal obstruction standing in their way. Much like the police exploitation of Beckert's crimes in *M* to crack down on the Berlin underworld, the Nazis would similarly make the case for martial law in the wake of the Reichstag fire of February 1933, which it has been alleged they set themselves, though the crime was blamed on the communists and considered an act of domestic terrorism. And as Lang draws a direct parallel between the criminal underworld and the Berlin police, historians such as Shirer have underlined the often-criminal histories—and practices—of various high ranking members of the Nazi party. Shirer writes, 'A conglomeration of pimps, murderers, homosexuals, alcoholics and blackmailers flocked to the party as if to a natural haven'.[8]

Part of *M*'s importance as a thriller and horror film is due to its similarly scathing comparison between different types of monstrosity: Beckert as a type of strangely sympathetic human monster; the mob as symbolic of the potential for monstrous violence in all humans; and the seamless conflation of cops and criminals. Dana Stevens writes,

> The police are everywhere, no longer associated with any abstract form of the Good in society, no longer protectors of any moral value: like Walter Benjamin's ghostly police in *Critique of Violence*, they are control itself, inhabiting a strange netherworld that is both above and below the law, never congruent with it. Power, violence and terror come from above *and* from below, until in the end the above meets the below, crushing everything in between.[9]

The film's original title was meant to be *Mörder Unter Uns* (*A Murderer Among Us*), which locates Beckert as just one of a faceless crowd and places 'the criminal as [a] contaminatory infestation'.[10] There is the implication that Beckert is a sympathetic figure because his impulses are beyond his control and are perhaps an inevitable result of life in Berlin. He exists in a nebulous grey area between police and criminals, and is later himself victimsed when he is hunted, captured, and faces death at the behest of the mothers of his own victims with their passionate thirst for vengeance. Lang suggests in these later scenes that the integration between working-class tenement families and the criminal underworld is a relatively seamless mingling; the families are better able to get justice from the underworld than with the aid of the police. The criminals are cleverer, better organised, and able to spread a ubiquitous, invisible net throughout the city as if they are an organic, even essential function of urban life.

Lang himself admitted to a fascination with real-life violence and criminality and their cinematic implications in a 1931 essay, 'My Film *M*: A Factual Report'. He discusses an interest in what would happen if criminals banded together and how this could be prevented; perhaps as a reflection on then-current events and the strengthening of Nazi forces. He describes *M* as a potential warning, a fantasy of the all-consuming violence that would result from mob rule:

> If this film based on factual reports helps to point an admonishing and warning finger at the unknown, lurking threat, the chronic danger emanating from the constant presence among us of compulsively and criminally inclined individuals, forming, so to speak, a latent potential that may devour our lives in flames—and especially the lives of the most helpless among us—and if the film also helps, perhaps, even to avert this danger, then it will have served its highest purpose and drawn the logical conclusion from the quintessential facts assembled in it.[11]

Perhaps this was an attempt to appease censors or a wary public and moralise the film's more unpleasant elements, to justify its subject matter of paedophilia and murder. But these lurid themes also belong to an important tradition of German literature and cinema. In the way that *M* can be seen to reflect the growing Nazi threat, Lang's use of monstrosity and violence is developed from the rich tradition of German expressionist cinema of the '10s and '20s, with its wealth of horror films, complicated villains and humanised monsters. The signature films of German expressionism—such as Robert Wiene's *The Cabinet of Dr. Caligari*, Paul Wegener's *Der Golem, wie er in die Welt kam / The Golem: How He Came into the World* (1920) or F.W. Murnau's *Nosferatu*—all mine the themes established by German Romanticism and Gothic literature.

## GERMAN ROMANTICISM AND EXPRESSIONIST HORROR

Historian Lotte Eisner states that 'Romanticism and Expressionism are interrelated'[12] and notes 'the inborn German liking for chiaroscuro and shadow'.[13] Certainly one of the trademark elements of expressionist art and cinema is the startling depiction of light and shadow, which would go on to influence American film noir and the emerging horror genre in Hollywood as droves of German filmmakers were forced to relocate in the late '20s and '30s. But there is also a thematic relationship between the films. Eisner writes,

> These works blithely married a morbid Freudianism and an Expressionistic exaltation to the romantic fantasies of Hoffmann and Eichendorff and to the tortured soul of contemporary Germany seemed, with their overtones of death, horror and nightmare, the reflection of its own grimacing image, offering a kind of release.[14]

Eisner refers to E.T.A. Hoffmann (1776-1822) and Joseph von Eichendorff (1788-1857), Prussian writers associated with the Romantic movement. While Eichendorff represents the strain of German Romanticism focused on an appreciation of nature and travelling, romantic love and themes of nostalgia, Hoffmann was influential in the emerging fields of fantasy and horror fiction, particularly on major figures like Edgar Allen Poe and Franz Kafka. Freud used Hoffmann's stories, such as 'The Sandman', in his theory of the uncanny. Hoffmann's use of reflections, dreams, madness and automata would feature heavily in German expressionist cinema, as well as throughout Lang's work. For example, the scene that fully introduces Lorre's Beckert involves him looking into a mirror, a common trope of Romanticism that likely represents his fragmented psyche.

In general, the German expressionist horror films either focus on a supernatural antagonist, as in *The Golem* or *Nosferatu*, or on a human one driven to madness. Eisner writes of the 'preoccupation with setting and atmosphere which was to be characteristic of the entire German cinema'[15] and describes these monstrous figures as representing both a mythic sense of isolation and even melancholy within the German psyche:

> The German soul instinctively prefers twilight to daylight. In *The Decline of the West* Oswald Spengler exalts the mist, the enigmatic chiaroscuro, the 'Kolossal,' and infinite solitude. The unlimited spaces cherished by the 'Faustian soul' of northern man are never clear and limpid but swathed in gloom; the Germanic Valhalla, symbol of a frightful solitude, is a grisaille [a decorative painting in grey monotone] ruled by unsociable heroes and hostile gods. Spengler asserts that solitaries are the only

men to know the 'cosmic experience'; they alone are capable of experiencing the inexpressible isolation and nostalgia of the forest.[16]

This theme of isolation represents a primary current in German expressionist horror films, which are often concerned with solitary killers or lonely monsters. While Count Orlok (Max Schreck) of Murnau's *Nosferatu* is one of the few expressionist horror villains to literally come from a remote forest location, many such characters are set apart from society if only in a psychological sense. In many ways, the essential expressionist horror film is Wiene's *The Cabinet of Dr. Caligari*—something Eisner also argues, going so far as to claim that it created the 'genre' of German expressionism itself.[17] The sinister Dr. Caligari (Werner Krauss) arrives at the village of Holstenwall with a carnival attraction in tow: a rail-thin somnambulist, Cesare (Conrad Veidt), who sleeps in a coffin and awakens during the carnival to answer the questions of audience members with uncanny accuracy, though he often makes ominous claims and predicts their deaths. Caligari has actually hypnotised Cesare to do his bidding and some nights he rises from sleep to murder those who have unwittingly offended Caligari.

Conrad Veidt's Cesare scales the iconic expressionist rooftops in *The Cabinet of Dr. Caligari*.

It is revealed that Caligari was the director of an insane asylum and is using one of his former patients to carry out his own mad aims. Caligari himself went insane after learning of a man who used a sleepwalker to commit crimes, and in this sense the conclusion of the narrative folds back in on itself, revealing new layers of madness among different characters: Cesare, Caligari and even Francis (Friedrich Feher), the story's narrator. According to Eisner and film historian Siegfried Kracauer, the original incarnation of the script lacked this framing story where not just Cesare and Caligari's actions are explained away with insanity, but also the protagonist's understanding of what has occurred. *The Cabinet of Dr. Caligari*'s main themes—man confronting his own violent impulses and base desires, doubling and madness—are the foundational tenets of expressionist horror cinema.

Eisner writes of the 'criminal insensibility and defiance of conventional morality which the Expressionists exalted',[18] and indeed many of these films are concerned with criminal acts, often murder. Cesare kills multiple people at Caligari's behest, which is prefigured by Max Mack's 1913 film *Der Andere / The Other*, where an attorney, sceptical of split personalities, suffers a traumatic accident and commits crimes in a state of sleepwalking. Both the 1913 version of *The Student of Prague*, directed by Stellan Rye and Paul Wegener, and the 1926 Henrik Galeen version follow an impulsive young student who has his reflection stolen as part of a questionable bargain; it becomes a pernicious doppelgänger that he must eventually kill, though he also winds up killing himself. Both the 1915 and 1920 versions of *The Golem* feature a creature meant to be protective, but who is twisted or corrupted for various reasons to become homicidal.

In Robert Reinert's non-horror film *Nerven / Nerves* (1919), the characters are driven to acts of hysteria and tormented by hallucinations from 'bouts of pathological rage' and 'bad heredity'; the film essentially ends with the message that humanity must go back to nature to start again because urban civilisation is too corrupt. Richard Oswald's horror anthology *Unheimliche Geschichten / Eerie Tales* (1919) follows a number of men haunted by their compulsions to murder or driven mad for various reasons. Murnau's lost film *Der Januskopf / The Head of Janus* (1920) follows a plot similar to *The Strange Case of Dr. Jekyll and Mr. Hyde*, where an unassuming scientist (Conrad Veidt, again) transforms into a base, violent double. In Arthur Robin's eerie melodrama *Schatten — Eine nächtliche Halluzination / Warning Shadows* (1923), a husband is driven mad and possibly driven to violence by his wife's flirtations with various suitors at a dinner party. Veidt returned for Robert Wiene's *Orlacs Hände / The Hands of Orlac* (1924), where a pianist survives an accident but undergoes an experimental transplant. He learns that his new hands belonged to a murderer and becomes obsessed with the idea that he will be consumed by the same violent impulses.

These are just a few examples of how the central titles of this loose genre were concerned with themes of madness and violence, but many of Veidt's tormented protagonists—particularly his starring role in *The Hands of Orlac*—represent the overarching theme that these characters are men driven by compulsions. *M*'s Beckert is certainly of their ilk. Many film historians have discussed this trend as being directly inspired by the aftermath of WWI, where mass casualties were experienced on an unprecedented scale. Many survivors were left physically deformed and psychologically traumatised. Eisner specifically posits this in relation to German literature. She writes,

> Mysticism and magic, the dark forces to which Germans have always been more than willing to commit themselves, had flourished in the face of death on the battlefields. The hecatombs of young men fallen in the flower of their youth seemed to nourish the grim nostalgia of the survivors. And the ghosts which had haunted the German Romantics revived, like the shades of Hades after draughts of blood.[19]

Clearly this is a climate in which mythic violence is brought into mundane life, as Lang himself experienced in '20s Berlin and brought to the screen in *M*, where the characters live in a city seemingly always on the brink of crime, murder and hysteria. This nightmarish depiction of urban spaces also has its roots in German expressionism: like *M*'s Berlin, the village of *The Cabinet of Dr. Caligari* is a place of stark shadows and disorienting angles. *Der Golem* similarly opens with a shot of children playing, but they are in front of the entrance to the Prague ghetto and the implication of violence and persecution is thick in the air. This is further explored in the melodrama and crime themes of the *Straßenfilm*, or 'street film', which I will discuss later.

These expressionistic cities and towns are also recognisable by the shared quality of their citizens, of the films' protagonists: as in German Romantic literature and many fairy tales, it is difficult to initially differentiate between friend and foe, hero or villain. Duality is a key theme in many of these early films. Eisner uses Caligari as an example, as he is 'both the eminent doctor and the fairground huckster', while Count Orlok is at once a creature of the undead and involved in a seemingly mundane activity: attempting to purchase real estate. Eisner writes,

For the Germans the demoniac side to an individual always has a middle-class counterpart. In the ambiguous world of the German cinema people are unsure of their identity and can easily lose it by the way. [...] The same morbid taste for split personality is also found in Fritz Lang's two Mabuse films and *M*.[20]

The doppelgänger is a more literal interpretation of this duality, where a person's 'shadow or reflection... takes on an independent existence and turns against its model'.[21] Mirrors and reflections are central to *M*, and in a sense there seem to be two Beckerts: the calm, assured child killer and the tormented loner. Like the great expressionistic monsters, such as *The Cabinet of Dr. Caligari*'s Cesare or *Nosferatu*'s Count Orlok, shadow, reflection and absence are critical visual symbols of his split identity and his monstrosity. When Beckert first appears on screen, it's as a silhouette over a wanted sign for the murderer, and one of the film's most iconic scenes features him staring at his fragmented reflection in the window of a shop.

*M* frequently depicts Beckert reflected in or shown through glass.

However, it is important to note that Lang is not quite tied to German expressionism as firmly as directors like Murnau or Wiene. Eisner writes, 'it would be wrong to consider his films as essentially Expressionistic'[22] and the director places a distinct emphasis on the psychological and on issues of law, order and power that seems to be a departure from the standard themes of expressionism. Dana Stevens writes that Lang's prewar themes include 'the mimetic confrontation between the lawless and the law, the emergence of the uncanny double, and most particularly, the terrible power of the written word, the letter'.[23] Writing is an important indicator of guilt, power and madness within both *M* and the Mabuse films, which marks a departure from the supernatural themes of many of the German expressionist movies like *The Student of Prague*, *Nosferatu* or *The Golem*. As in *The Cabinet of Dr. Caligari*, Lang's monsters are all too human.

In *The Cabinet of Dr. Caligari*, Cesare is sympathetic because he is a slave, a bound creature twisted, brainwashed and imprisoned by his creator, much as Paul Orlac of *The Hands of Orlac* is marked by his mutilation and the resultant surgery and believes he has lost agency over his own flesh. Beckert similarly represents this duality between sympathetic victim and monstrous killer, except in his case there is no external party responsible for his deeds, which horrify criminals and police alike. Stevens writes: 'Lorre's murderer is that absolute other, abhorred by both the law and by the outside-the-law, vowed to a destruction that exceeds his powers "as creature".'[24]

Considering that *M* was Lang's first horror-thriller, this characterisation seems deliberate, particularly because the early years of his career were prolific and, in many ways, *M* and 1933's *The Testament of Dr. Mabuse* seem like the culmination of everything he had been working towards, particularly after so much experimentation with genre. He effectively helped create the cinematic crime film, the fantasy epic, the science fiction epic and dystopian cinema, before escaping Germany to head West and produce some of the most important anti-fascist films of the '30s and '40s, as well as shape the film noir cycle of the '40s and '50s.

## LANG'S SILENT CINEMA

Lang's first period, from 1919 to 1929, was concerned with silent films: of these, *Halbblut* (1919) and *Der Herr der Liebe* (1919) are lost, while *Harakiri* (1919) and *Das wandernde Bild / The Wandering Shadow* (1920) are relatively standard melodramatic tales of troubled women. *Vier um die Frau / Four Around a Woman* (1921) continued this theme, as a husband becomes obsessed with the idea that his wife is cheating on him and he begins spying on her. These themes of espionage and paranoia would become a constant throughout his work, while the plot of two-part adventure-thriller *Die Spinnen / The Spiders* (1919) revolves around the idea of an underworld criminal gang; Lang would return to this repeatedly throughout his German films.

He followed *Die Spinnen* with early masterpieces like *Der müde Tod / Destiny* (1921), a fatalistic, three-part film about a woman's attempts to beat death and reclaim her lost lover, and *Dr. Mabuse the Gambler*, a visionary film about paranoia, corruption and evil. Dr. Mabuse (Rudolf Klein-Rogge) is a mastermind who uses hypnosis and surveillance to control the criminal underworld, while a stubborn prosecutor (Bernhard Goetzke) attempts to track him down. This is a unique glimpse of Europe between the two World Wars and has also been read by many critics, beginning notably with Siegfried Kracauer, as an early portent of the rise of Nazi Germany. Mabuse is perhaps cinema's first master villain and provides an unsettling introduction to his emerging, real-life totalitarian counterparts, such as Hitler, Franco and Stalin.

Rudolf Klein-Rogge mesmerizes as Dr. Mabuse in one of his many guises.

Based on a novel by Norbert Jacques and penned by Thea von Harbou, Lang's new wife (they were married in the same year as the film's release), this was to be the first of Lang's three-film *Mabuse* series with other directors later taking up the mantle. *Mabuse* is one of the early cinematic examples of the arch-villain, following characters from film serials and earlier serialised fiction like Fantomas and Fu Manchu. At more than four hours, *Dr. Mabuse the Gambler* is more correctly thought of as a serial than a feature-length film by current standards. As Nicole Brenez writes, 'The figure of Mabuse presented in 1922 is in fact so fantastic and archetypal that, for both Lang and his audience, it could have consequently referred to the most menacing of real-life autocrats, to the master of the historical moment. For what first mobilizes Lang is not a man, a singular being, but a phenomenon.'[25]

This film follows Dr. Mabuse as he uses his powers of disguise, hypnosis and mind-control to spread his criminal web across Berlin. He uses a network of henchmen—including murderers, drug addicts, thugs and even a cabaret dancer—to further his ends, which include everything from elaborate stock market heists to cheating and entrapping locals at the gambling dens, over which he has near total control. He targets a young industrialist (Paul Richter), the heir to a fortune, just as a prosecutor, Nobert von Wenk (Bernhard Goetzke), begins to string together some of Mabuse's crimes and build a case that centres on two women: Cara Carozza (Aude Egede-Nissen), a besotted cabaret dancer under Mabuse's control, and the Countess Told (Gertrude Welcker), who becomes the object of Mabuse's insane desire.

*Dr. Mabuse the Gambler* effectively captures the sense of moral depravity that came to characterise Weimar Germany, particularly seedy Berlin, and much of the film is set in gambling dens or nightclubs. Lang seems to be targeting the mass confusion that allowed criminals, gangs and thugs to take over Germany one street brawl or political seat at a time throughout the '20s—though, importantly, as in *M*, he draws no real distinction between them. Lang himself said of the film, 'It grew out of its time. Germany was a place where every type of excess was encountered and the film reflected the inflationary hysteria, the anarchistic streak, the despair and vices of the time.'[26]

Mabuse, like many who would rise in the ranks of the Nazi party in the years to come, is purely an opportunist and feels no devotion for any particular political cause. There is the sense that Mabuse is able to shift, chameleon-like, between so many different layers of German society, because of the lack of distinct political or economic identities; everyone—from the working class to the aristocracy—had lost their place and as a result, is a likely target for Mabuse and his network of criminals. And in German, the 'spieler' of the film's original title, *Dr. Mabuse der Spieler*, implies more than just 'gambler'. 'Spielen' literally means 'to play', and the world connotes that Mabuse is a player, a gambler and even an actor, his crimes and machinations a grand performance, which culminate with a chilling scene of group hypnosis.

This obsession with costume, ritual and spectacle—combined with themes of voyeurism and surveillance, needing to see and be seen—represent the gradual slide into totalitarianism that was occurring at that very moment in German society. Nicole Brenez writes:

> Through the figure of the arch-criminal, the film treats modern tyranny as it is, factually, at the moment Lang portrays it: a 'conspiratorial society.' Hitler, in a memo dated October 22, 1922, said: 'We will create a movement that will rouse the most fanatical force and the most brutal sense of determination, that will be ready at all moments to counter a terrorism ten times greater than that of Marxism.'[27]

Many of Lang's later film noir and crime efforts deal with the type of inherent corruption already present in *Dr. Mabuse the Gambler*—whether it is in the media, legal system, or in mob justice—and with the machinery of society that turns apparently decent people into criminals and murderers. The themes that came to obsess him in his later American films, and which took their fullest form in *M*, such as surveillance, revenge, mob justice, media corruption and hypocrisy, first emerged in *Dr. Mabuse the Gambler* and the science fiction epic *Metropolis*, where a futuristic, urban society has transformed the working class into tormented slaves. Somewhat similarly, *Spies* focuses on widespread social corruption and the theme of an underworld criminal conspiracy. Featuring much of the creative team behind Lang's lesser seen but still visionary sci-fi epic *Frau im Mond / Woman in the Moon* (1929), *Spies* follows an intelligence agent ordered to take down the leader of an international espionage organisation, who is hiding in plain sight, just like Mabuse. His network of spies and assassins have penetrated all levels of society.

*Spies* is set in a fundamentally corrupt world, also seen in the *Dr. Mabuse* films and *M*, ruled by all-powerful cabals and choked by paranoia and oppression. And like the *Dr. Mabuse* films and *M*, *Spies* is fixated on death and violence in a way that Lang would hardly have been allowed to explore in Hollywood at that time: multiple suicides, assassinations and murders, and a scene of torture by black leather-clad agents that would eerily foreshadow Gestapo practices in just a few short years. These elements are a strong example of how these early titles, particularly *Dr. Mabuse the Gambler* and *Spies*, represent the evolution of Lang's career as a director—not only in terms of what he was able to accomplish stylistically, with his manipulation of German expressionist tropes, but particularly in terms of how his themes were gradually crystallised, drawing him inexorably towards M, which exists within the same loose universe as these films. Where Dr. Mabuse is often read as the embodiment of post-WWI depression and the inflation crisis of the early '20s, Beckert can similarly be interpreted as the physical manifestation of the events of 1929-1931: crippling economic and political turmoil that leads to violence and mob rule.

**FOOTNOTES**

5. The Metropolitan Museum of Art. 'Berlin Street.' http://www.metmuseum.org/toah/works-of-art/63.220/
6. William L. Shirer, *The Rise and Fall of the Third Reich: A History of Nazi Germany*. Simon & Schuster, 2011. p. 117.
7. Ibid., p. 136.
8. Ibid., p. 122.
9. Dana Stevens (1993), p. 64.
10. Ibid., p. 64.
11. Fritz Lang. 'My Film M: A Factual Report.' https://www.criterion.com/current/posts/1457-my-film-m-a-factual-report.
12. Lotte Eisner, *The Haunted Screen: Expressionism in the German Cinema and the Influence of Max Reinhardt*. Secker & Warburg, 1973. P. 15.
13. Ibid., p. 17.
14. Ibid.
15. Ibid., p. 43.
16. Ibid., p. 51.
17. Ibid., p. 27.
18. Ibid., p. 27.
19. Ibid., p. 9.
20. Ibid., p. 110.
21. Ibid., p. 40.
22. Ibid., p. 93.
23. Dana Stevens (1993), p. 71.
24. Ibid., p. 75.
25. Nicole Brenez, 'Symptom, Exhibition, Fear: Representations of Terror in the German Work of Fritz Lang.' *A Companion to Fritz Lang*. Ed. Joe McElhaney. Wiley Blackwell, 2015. p. 64

26. Barry Keith Grant, *Fritz Lang: Interviews*. University Press of Mississippi, 2003. p. 89.
27. Nicole Brenez (2015), p. 64.

# Chapter Two: In the Hall of the Mountain King

> Slay him!
> May I hack him on the fingers?
> May I tug him by the hair?
> Hu, hey, let me bite him in the haunches!
> Shall he be boiled into broth and bree to me
> Shall he roast on a spit or be browned in a stewpan?
> —Edvard Grieg, *Peer Gynt*

One of *M*'s most innovative elements is Lang's use of a serial killer as a protagonist, a previously unheard of convention in horror films or crime thrillers. Beckert is the undeniable focus of the film and stands as a lone individual character in the midst of an essentially nameless mob. He is at once a sort of victimised antihero, hunted and persecuted—a character type that would later appear in film noir—while also serving as the vilest of antagonists: a child killer. Of course, *M* was not the first film to feature a murderer in a prominent role, though most of these earlier titles are not horror movies or thrillers, but crime films or serials. These titles often explored criminal gangs or shadowy, evil masterminds who served more as cyphers than fully realised characters.

An early silent example is the Portuguese short film *Os Crimes de Diogo Alves / The Crimes of Diogo Alves* (1909; remade in 1911), which focuses on the exploits of a real-life criminal. This was also generally the central theme for the episodic and often quite lurid crime serials of the '10s and '20s. Those made by French director Louis Feuillade were some of the most popular, such as *Fantômas* (1913) or *Les vampires* (1915), though, utterly unlike Beckert and more akin to Dr. Mabuse, Fantômas is ubiquitous and changeable. As a master of disguise, he constantly takes on new faces and identities. His criminal acts are motivated less by the psychological torment that possesses Beckert and more by an all-consuming amorality that makes every type of crime attractive to him: murder, certainly, but also theft, embezzlement, blackmail, kidnapping and so on.

A lot of early horror—such as the silent short films of Georges Méliès—was supernaturally themed, but psychological terror became an increasingly popular subject. Probably the most popular horror story to put a killer front and centre in the narrative, which inspired a lot of direct adaptations as well as similarly themed, loose interpretations, was Robert Louis Stevenson's 1886 Gothic novel, *The Strange Case of Dr. Jekyll and Mr. Hyde*. This famous tale of a doctor whose personality is split by his scientific experiments was first adapted in the United States in 1908, though that film is now lost, but was a popular subject in the 1910s-20s. It was filmed six times in various countries, though sometimes blended with elements of Oscar Wilde's *The Picture of Dorian Gray* (1890), the period's other famous study of man's warring impulses.

Like *M*, the most well-regarded of these early silent productions, 1920's *Dr. Jekyll and Mr. Hyde*, was driven by a charismatic central performance: in this case, from John Barrymore. The film's premise is that the benevolent, if austere, Dr. Jekyll becomes transfixed by pronouncements from his future father-in-law (Brandon Hurst) that 'a man cannot destroy the savage in him by denying its impulses. The only way to get rid of a temptation is to yield to it.' There is the tacit admission that even Jekyll possesses these impulses and he begins an experiment attempting to divide these 'good' and 'evil' natures, with disastrous results. Arguably the most famous sound version of the film was released the same year as *M*: Rouben Mamoulian's *Dr. Jekyll and Mr. Hyde*, starring Fredric March as the well-meaning doctor whose experiments are driven by his own uncontrollable desire for his fiancée (Rose Hobart). Upping the sadism from the 1920 version of the film, it is implied that March's Hyde is sexually and physically abusing a downtrodden dancer (Miriam Hopkins) that Jekyll once rescued.

Of course, there were also German versions of the same story, such as Max Mack's *Ein seltsamer Fall* (1914) and his previously mentioned *The Other*, as well as Murnau's *Der Januskopf*. Lang certainly would have been familiar with these and there is an obvious link between Conrad Veidt's tortured protagonists and the impulses that drive Beckert to madness and violence. And in terms of other German cinema to feature murderers, Paul Leni's *Wachsfigurenkabinett / Waxworks* (1924) was one of the first to depict a serial killer on screen. In this episodic film, a writer (William Dieterle) imagines stories for various villainous figures in a wax museum and one segment focuses on Jack the Ripper (Werner Krauss). Leni would help to establish a certain type of horror-thriller after he relocated to the US in 1927, at the behest of Universal Studios producer Carl Laemmle, when he directed *The Cat and the Canary* (1927). This film, along with Leni's

Frederic March's Mr. Hyde true nature is revealed when he torments a dancer (Miriam Hopkins) in a scene with surprisingly strong sexually suggestive content for the period.

loose follow up, The Last Warning (1929), are whodunnits that combine elements of mystery, horror and black comedy.

In The Cat and the Canary—likely influenced by Roland West's slightly earlier film The Bat (1926), which follows a similar premise—a young heiress (Laura La Plante) will only inherit the fortune of her distant, eccentric uncle if she can be declared sane by a doctor. But she must first survive a night in a spooky old mansion, while a serial killer nicknamed 'the Cat', who 'tears his victims like they were canaries', is on the loose after having escaped the local asylum. The focus of the film is clearly La Plante's vulnerable young woman and, as with so many of these 'old dark house' films, as they would come to be known, the culprit is really someone close to the protagonist hoping to claim the inheritance themselves, and not an anonymous killer motivated by dark sexual urges.

In terms of Hollywood, most of the films from the '20s to feature killers often emphasised psychological themes, such as many of Lon Chaney's roles where he was cast as a sympathetic—or at least charismatic—figure capable of great violence. While he is largely remembered for his talent with special make-up effects as the titular monstrous characters in *The Hunchback of Notre Dame* (1923) and *The Phantom of the Opera* (1925), he also played a series of grotesquely mutilated protagonists obsessed with revenge (or even just fixated on crime in general) in films like *The Penalty* (1920), the Grand Guignolesque *While Paris Sleeps* (1923), *The Unholy Three* (1925) and *The Unknown* (1927). While we are not explicitly meant to identify with his characters in these films—and they all come to their own violent ends—Chaney helped set the stage for Lorre's Beckert by making these characters sympathetic and deeply compelling even in the midst of plotting or committing horrible acts.

A final theme from this period worth mentioning is the blending of Edgar Allan Poe's influence into films that could best be described as dark melodrama, but generally focused on a protagonist driven to madness and violence by a series of seemingly mundane (i.e. not supernatural) events. D.W. Griffith's early films *The Sealed Room* (1909) and *The Avenging Conscience: Or 'Thou Shalt Not Kill'* (1914) are both riffs on this, in turn borrowing from Poe's stories 'The Cask of Amontillado' and 'The Tell-Tale Heart'. One of the most important examples of this theme, though it's largely forgotten by contemporary audiences, is James Young's *The Bells* (1926) starring Lionel Barrymore. Based on an 1871 play by Leopold Davis Lewis, a vehicle for Henry Irving, the story follows an innkeeper who murders a wealthy man out of greed, but is tormented into madness by guilt over his crime.

Beckert's outburst at the conclusion of *M*, his tormented confession and plea for his life, finds its origins in *The Bells*. While the innkeeper does not commit murder because of a psychological compulsion, but because he wants to clear his mounting debts and elevate his social status, both characters are plagued by similar feelings of guilt and become similarly hounded by external and internal forces. Guilt is a major theme in Poe's writing, and in gothic literature in general, and the tension between a character's compulsion to commit crimes while also lamenting their own actions is a potent source of horror in his writings and the films they influenced. In this sense, *M* is linked back to this vein of Gothic horror, even while it discards other popular tropes of the genre like crumbling castles and ancestral curses.

Poe focused on this theme in famous stories like 'The Black Cat' and 'The Tell-Tale Heart', and more widely featured narrators who justify their own horrific violence in tales such as 'The Cask of Amontillado'. *M* is one of the earliest films to borrow this trope of the unstable narrator, on which Poe frequently relied. Using 'The Tell-Tale Heart' as a key example, Dawn B. Sova writes:

> Poe explores several themes in the narrative, including those of sanity versus insanity, guilt versus innocence. [...] The mental state of the narrator is at issue from the first line of the story—'True!—nervous—very, very dreadfully nervous had I been and am, but why will you say that I am mad?'[28]

Beckert is not necessarily an unreliable narrator, as he is immediately introduced as a child killer. Throughout the film, Lang depicts him alternately as a calculating predator, in control of his actions—as is the protagonist of 'The Cask of Amontillado'—and as a man driven by monstrous impulses beyond his control who is slowly succumbing to madness. Beckert's raving monologue at the end of the film is certainly not the speech of a measured, rational man, and by the conclusion of *M*, he has transformed completely into a desperate, hunted animal.

Like Poe, who frequently relied on human psychology as a source of horror, Lang's long career often focused on various aspects of a theme that might be described as 'man's compulsion toward violence'. While his previously mentioned early films often focus on the criminal impulse and its effect on society, several of his later films explore violence by political necessity, such as *Man Hunt* (1941) and *Hangmen Also Die!* (1943), or pathological violent impulses as in *Secret Beyond the Door* (1947), *While the City Sleeps* (1956) and *Beyond a Reasonable Doubt* (1956). *M* was Lang's first full immersion into the world of abnormal psychology, though he arguably flirts with this topic in *Dr. Mabuse the Gambler* and *Spies*. His abandonment of supernatural and science fiction horror themes so popular during the period with films like *Dracula* (1931), *Frankenstein* (1931) and *The Mummy* (1932), helped create a cinematic subgenre that merges together horror and suspense. His contemporaries like Alfred Hitchcock and Robert Siodmak tread similar territory, and the serial killer film in general, as a subgenre, largely exists in this space in more contemporary cinema through directors like Brian De Palma and David Fincher.

The source of this is also undeniably Edgar Allan Poe, who made early forays not just into horror, but also into detective fiction through his character of C. Auguste Dupin, the first literary detective. The character appeared in stories like 'Murders in the Rue Morgue' and 'The Purloined Letter', among others. Like Sherlock Holmes, he's an early example of the 'gentleman detective', and was not a police officer, but an independent investigator, even a hobbyist, with a knack for getting into the minds of criminals. In 'Murders in the Rue Morgue' he solves a gruesome 'locked room' mystery and uncovers that the culprit is a monstrous ape. The purpose of the story is undeniably the exercise of solving a murder and Dupin's method, 'ratiocination', is the crux of the plot and takes primacy over the murders themselves. Similarly, in 'The Mystery of Marie Rogêt', Dupin solves the murder of a young woman dumped in the river.

The emphasis in Poe's few detective stories and the later, popular fiction of writers like Sir Arthur Conan Doyle is on the detective's method: who committed the crime and how, and how did the detective in question laboriously trace this path of evidence and narrow the pool of suspects? Where Lang further innovates is that *M* is not a *whodunnit*, but a *whydunnit*. The narrative establishes the identity of the killer or criminal early on and focuses on his motivations and the consequences for his actions. This allows Lang to focus not on the detective or on the victims of a crime, but on the character of the murderer. Brian Duffy writes:

> The move from a whodunnit to a whydunnit seems at first sight to shift the inquiry away from identity, as the goal of the investigation is no longer to determine the identity of the individual. But this latter, traditional preoccupation of detective fiction has more to do with identification than identity, with simple naming rather than with a radical inquiry into the philosophical and existential dimensions of the notions of personal identity and selfhood. Paradoxically, then, it is precisely in moving from a whodunnit to a whydunnit, with the subsequent shifting of focus from a death to a life, that the more profound implications of the concept of identity may be explored.[29]

*M* is a complex and often horrifying examination of the identity of a killer, stripped of its emphasis on mystery and detection. This theme would go on to become a major component of film noir, which Lang both heavily influenced with his early German films, and also shaped as an active participant as a Hollywood director once he relocated to American shores a few years after *M*. It's also important to examine *M*'s use of the murderer as protagonist—and this focus on whydunnit rather than whodunnit—

in contrast with the other most important serial killer film from the period: Alfred Hitchcock's *The Lodger: A Story of the London Fog* (1927).

## COMPARISONS TO *THE LODGER*

Hitchcock's third feature film, though one that he generally regarded as his creative debut, establishes many of the themes that would define his career: a blonde leading lady, murder most foul, and a 'wrong man' scenario. Hitchcock biographer Donald Spoto writes, 'Hitchcock has revealed his psychological attraction to the association between sex and murder, between ecstasy and death.'[30] Based on the novel of the same name by Marie Belloc Lowndes, the plot blends elements of the thriller and horror genres to relate the tale of a mysterious killer known as the Avenger—a loose reinterpretation of Jack the Ripper—who murders blondes on Tuesday nights.

The protagonist, Daisy (June Tripp), is a model; her friends at work begin to dye or cover their blonde locks, while Daisy refuses to take the killings seriously. She lives with her parents, who take in lodgers, and their latest is a strange young man (Ivor Novello) who keeps to himself and exhibits some odd behavior, such as his request that the portraits of blonde women in his room be removed. But he and Daisy develop a mutual attraction, despite the fact that she has a police officer boyfriend, Joe (Malcolm Keen). Unfortunately for Daisy, signs point towards the lodger's guilt, particularly when he is found to be out of the house on the nights of the killings. Daisy's boyfriend arrests him, but Daisy is determined to help him clear his name.

Ultimately, the lodger is indeed proven to be innocent and it is suggested that he and Daisy will go on to live happily ever after. This ending, required by the studio because of the presence of star Ivor Novello, differs both from the novel and from Hitchcock's intended conclusion—something that would be resurrected in Hitchcock's *Suspicion* (1941), where a woman (Joan Fontaine) believes her husband (Cary Grant) is trying to kill her. In Lowndes' book, as in some of the later adaptations like John Brahm's 1944 version starring Laird Cregar, the lodger does turn out to be the murderer. Hitchcock departed from this initial conclusion and was planning to make his ending quite ambiguous, where the lodger's guilt or innocence is never conclusively revealed. In the film's actual ending, there is a glimmer of this ambiguity; while the lodger is persecuted and nearly killed by an enraged mob, he is exonerated just in time because another man has been arrested for the crimes. Hitchcock frustrates conventions by never showing us this other, 'real' killer, leaving the ambiguity somewhat in place.

Ivor Novello skulks in the fog in *The Lodger*.

There is no doubt that through *The Lodger*, Hitchcock came into his own as a director and discovered the genre that would become his oeuvre—and the one that he would irrevocably alter. In the famous interview he did with Francois Truffaut, Hitchcock himself said that *The Lodger* was 'the first true Hitchcock picture'.[31] Philip Kemp writes:

> We are so used to thinking of Alfred Hitchcock as the Master of Suspense that it comes as a surprise to realize that he was nearly a decade into his career as a director before he definitively latched on to the genre that was to become his stock-in-trade. [...] Of the seventeen features Hitchcock directed before *The Man Who Knew Too Much*, nine of them silent, only three can be classified as suspense thrillers: *The Lodger: A Story of the London Fog* (1927), *Blackmail* (1929—his first sound film), and *Number Seventeen* (1932), with its cheerful throwaway nonsense.[32]

Lang, similarly, began his career by exploring a variety of genres, settling primarily on thrillers with *M*, and the parallel between the two films is fascinating, especially in terms of the roles these films played in the careers of their directors. Nearly a decade ahead of Hitchcock in years and experience, Lang was undoubtedly an influence on the younger British director. And perhaps more than any of Hitchcock's other thrillers, the influence of German expressionism is clear in *The Lodger*'s visual world; Hitchcock himself spoke about this in his interview with Truffaut. But what is really striking about comparing the two films side by side is that despite their similarities—both are set in major cities, concern a serial killer or potential serial killer murdering because of an implied sexual compulsion, and feature a conclusion with a violent mob—the dramatically different narrative choices result in overwhelmingly different films.

To begin with, there is again the difference between the whodunit and the whydunit. As a whodunnit, *The Lodger* focuses on the identity of the killer and spends much of its running time stressing the lodger's likely guilt, while confusing the issue by making Daisy fall in love with him. Lesley Brill writes of

> Hitchcock's self-conscious treatment of the mystery genre, the playfulness with which he treats its more conspicuous conventions and his systematic manipulation of the audience's expectations. [...] Hitchcock relentlessly uses the conventions of the murder mystery to cast suspicion upon the Lodger.[33]

Hitchcock spent much of his subsequent career deconstructing, subverting and reforming these conventions in films like *Rear Window* (1954) and *Psycho*, and his seeming obsession with the 'wrong man' trope is bound up with the innocent but persecuted protagonist's need to uncover the actually guilty party.

Lang takes the opposite approach, both in *M* and in the majority of his later thrillers. With very few exceptions, such as *Secret Beyond the Door* or *Beyond a Reasonable Doubt*, Lang often establishes the identity of the killer (or killers) early in the film. Thus, these narratives are not concerned with whodunnit, but explore the killer's motivations and the ways in which they are brought to justice (or not), and often how this pursuit of justice transforms and often corrupts other characters within the narrative.

Lang and Hitchcock both seem deeply suspicious of law enforcement and the legal system, but also of large groups of people in general. Hitchcock examined this throughout his career in subtler ways, as in films like *The Lady Vanishes* (1938) or *The Birds* (1963), but rarely as overtly as in *The Lodger*. Brill writes:

> Hitchcock's famously unenthusiastic view of the police appears clearly in this early film, as does his less well-known but more consistent demophobia. In a Hitchcock film any group of people larger than roughly half a dozen registers as a mob—conformist, unimaginative, inhumane.[34]

The fact that both films take place in cities is not a coincidence and both seem to posit that deviance is an unavoidable result of urban life. Probably their greatest overt similarity is in this portrayal of toxic urban environments and the implicit link drawn between the media, voyeurism and perversion. In both films, news of the homicides is conveyed to the audience—and to the respective residents of London and Berlin—by newspapers, advertisements and posters. Brill writes of *The Lodger*:

> While the film, like the media it portrays, exploits the sensational appeal of homicide, it also brings to its subject a complex personal and social understanding quite unlike media accounts. The voyeuristic eyes suggested by the rear windows of the newspaper van represent only too well the public perspective on violent crimes.[35]

This sensationalism is an aspect not only of *The Lodger*, but also of *M*, and in both films the masses are attracted and repulsed by reports of these murders. The mounting frenzy associated with the continuing crimes is related to the fact that in either case, the police fail to locate a suspect in time. This climaxes in a violent mob pursuing the protagonist and nearly tearing him limb from limb. Violence thus becomes a communal act.

Lang is openly critical and even dismissive of the police in *M*, where they're only vaguely defined characters. On the other hand, Hitchcock places Joe, Daisy's boyfriend, in a central role. He's effectively the third member of a love triangle, of which Daisy is the focal point, and despite his unspoken role as the film's moral centre, Joe has a dark edge. In an early scene, he has a gag with handcuffs, which has a sadistic sexual connotation, and he is shown to be quite controlling of Daisy. And as much as Daisy's fetishised 'golden hair' would recur throughout Hitchcock's career, so would Joe's character in one form or another. Kemp writes: 'The overpossessive and morally ambiguous policeman boyfriend, another recurrent Hitchcock character (*Blackmail*; *Sabotage*, 1936; *Shadow of a Doubt*, 1943; *Notorious*, 1946), makes his first appearance in *The Lodger*.'[36] It's clear that this is a world where men, even the film's two central romantic leads, are capable of sexual obsession, perversion and even violence.

This is another way in which *The Lodger* and *M* are so divergent; *M* lacks any romantic plot, though Lang didn't shy away from this theme throughout his career. Typically his cinematic relationships took on roles secondary to the central plot, as in *Spies* or

*Woman on the Moon*, and the romantic relationships of Lang's films after *M* often have nasty undertones or violent conclusions, as in *Woman in the Window* (1944), *Scarlet Street* (1945), *Secret Beyond the Door* and *Human Desire* (1954), among many others. While Hitchcock's sexual obsession often resolves into a happy ending—even in the case of *The Lodger*, *Shadow of a Doubt*, *Notorious*, *Spellbound* (1945) and *Marnie*—Lang generally lacks such romantic conclusions.

Much of this hinges on the difference between Lang's standard protagonists and Hitchcock's. The titular lodger remains a mysterious figure with just enough hints of his dark past to make him seem misunderstood, tormented, even tragic. This is a type Hitchcock would play with in later films like *Rebecca* (1940), *Suspicion* and *Frenzy*. In essence, the lodger is defined by his ambiguity and this also seems to be the source of Daisy's attraction to him. Richard Allen wonders: 'Is the Lodger an aristocratic, amateur sleuth seeking to capture the criminal who murdered his sister or is he that criminal himself? Is he a figure of threat or sympathy? Is he a gentleman or sexual predator?'[37] Lorre's Beckert, on the other hand, is a transparent figure and despite his strange charisma, there is no mystery or romantic ambiguity to his character.

## Peter Lorre: Murderer and Matinee Idol

Unlike in *The Lodger*, *M*'s murderer is the centrepiece of the film and arguably the sole fully realised character in the entire script. It is Lorre's charisma and his ability to portray Beckert as both predatory and victimised, villainous and pathetic, that adds so much nuance to the role. Dara Waldron writes that 'Lorre's is one of the great "criminal" performances in film history'.[38] Lorre portrays Beckert not as some villain existing on a scale of black and white moral absolutes, but 'as the pawn of some cosmic struggle'.[39] Acknowledging this fact in his discussions of the film in the years after its release, Lang described Lorre's performance as the greatest of the actor's life and one of the best in film history. Regardless, tensions between the two men were often high on set, as Lorre was then an inexperienced film actor, with numerous stage credits but little else by 1930. Prior to his starring turn in *M*, he had an uncredited appearance in the comedy *Die verschwundene Frau / The Missing Wife* (1929) and a small role in *Der weiße Teufel / The White Devil* (1930), a Russian-themed historical drama. *M* would change his life.

The experience was apparently a trying one for the young actor. Due to his contract, he had to wait months without taking on any other projects for the shooting of *M* to begin. Once it did, Lang was apparently quite cruel to him, ensuring the production was physically taxing and Lorre was often battered and bruised at the end of the day. It was thus an exhausted, worn down Lorre, driven to the edge of hysteria, who delivered the film's signature monologue about evil, morality and compulsion. This final sequence underlines how little control Beckert has over his own impulses, but unlike some of the later serial killers of cinema, he is plagued by remorse over his deeds, crying, 'I can't help myself! I haven't any control over this evil thing that's inside me.' He claims that the children never leave him, implying that he is tormented by their ghosts, which adds a further edge of psychosis and paranoia to the proceedings.

Peter Lorre peers into his own abyss as Hans Beckert.

Lorre's physicality adds a particular complexity to the role. Short in stature and with a round, baby face—particularly during the filming of *M* when he was still in his twenties—his more childlike characteristics and often eccentric features add a cartoonish, even fairytale-like component to Beckert that is only enhanced by the tune Lang chose to accompany the character: 'In the Hall of the Mountain King'. One of the first instances of a filmmaker using a leitmotif, typically a traditional component of opera, the whistled song that introduces Beckert also hints at Lang's interest in myth, which he explored at its fullest with Die Nibelungen a few years prior in 1924. Taken from Henrik Ibsen's play Peer Gynt, 'In the Hall of the Mountain King' is part of the incidental music composed by Edvard Grieg.

The satirical, surreal play, which borrowed from Norwegian fairy tales and folklore, follows the titular Peer Gynt, an aimless dreamer. He's banished from his community and wanders to the mountains, where he has a number of adventures, as well as some fateful encounters with trolls. 'In the Hall of the Mountain King' accompanies his journey to meet the troll king of the mountain, whose court is populated with trolls, goblins and other creatures. Because Peer Gynt has aroused the affections of the king's daughter, the court sings about dismembering and cooking him: 'Shall he be boiled into broth and bree to me? Shall he roast on a spit or be browned in a stewpan?' It seems intentional that Beckert's theme would subtly evoke both whimsical fantasy and horrific violence.

This seeming contradiction is at the heart of Lorre's performance. Sarah Thomas writes that his particular theatrical experience helped him create such a nuanced performance: 'Lorre's practical theatrical training, in experimental productions and as part of avant-garde companies around Europe, had encouraged the development of a multi-layered acting style that could be described as "dualistic".'[40] Lorre's work with seminal playwright Bertolt Brecht was also a contributing factor. Brecht pioneered a technique known as the *Verfremdungseffekt*, or 'alienation effect', where an actor's words and gestures are meant to draw attention to the fact that the audience is watching a theatrical performance, aiding in a presumably more in-depth critical analysis of the material by preventing the viewer from getting lost in a play or film's fictional world. Lorre's physicality as Beckert is often non-naturalistic, bolstered by a use of shadows, minimal dialogue and unusual camera angles. Lorre seems to be constantly displaying and removing a series of masks that he wears as a performer, but also that Beckert wears throughout the narrative.

Another important connection between Lang, Lorre and Brecht is the playwright's influence on German theatre and cinema through his depictions of criminality. Stephen Brockmann writes:

> Lang's depiction of criminality and criminal organizations is not fundamentally different from Bertolt Brecht's even more radical depiction of criminality in his opera *Die*

> *Dreigroschenoper* (*The Threepenny Opera*, 1928), made into a film by G.W. Pabst in 1931, the same year as *M*. For Brecht—just as for Lang in *M*—organized criminality is merely one more form of capitalist enterprise. Brecht's opera had also featured the association between organized criminality and organized beggars, and it is likely that Lang was influenced by it.[41]

While I will more fully explore the connection between *The Threepenny Opera* and *M* in a later chapter, both films provide scathing commentary about German society through the use of criminal characters. But while *The Threepenny Opera* follows an anarchic criminal and antihero who leads his own gang and is a something of a local celebrity, Lang and Lorre manage to turn their own antihero into a sympathetic figure isolated from social interaction. Lorre biographer Stephen Youngkin writes: 'Committed to explaining the murderer's motives, he presented Beckert not as a monster but as a divided human being whose darker side acts independently of his will.'[42] Lorre himself recognised the significance of the character—particularly in terms of the enduring legacy of *M*—and said, 'I was a murderer, but I was a matinee idol'.[43]

The character of Beckert would go on to shape Lorre's entire career and he was often typecast to loosely fit within this mold. Sarah Thomas writes:

> More than any other role, Beckert has come to be seen as the character which had the biggest impact on Lorre's life—both in terms of his continued employment in the film industry and also in the way that this character contributed to the development of Lorre's otherwise extra-filmic persona. [...] Hollywood either cast Lorre as a pervert, a serial killer, a sexual threat or an outsider.[44]

For the next two decades of his career, he was generally relegated to such roles—often to great effect—but he would never again reach the heights he soared with Lang. Though he acted in a handful of films in Germany in 1932 and 1933, his next major performance was after he temporarily relocated to England to appear in Hitchcock's *The Man Who Knew Too Much* (1934). In the film, a couple's daughter is kidnapped when they accidentally stumble across a criminal gang led by Abbott (Lorre), notable for his accent, prominent facial scar and white streak in his hair. Farran Smith Nehme connects the film directly to *M*, stating that it was specifically Lorre's performance for Lang that made Hitchcock determined to hire:

This Lorre character is a reversal of the one he plays in *M*. Abbott isn't a man who preys on children, he's a child who preys on adults. [...] Lorre merges the Continent and the underworld to create a unique breed of refined psychopath. His silkily evil performance dominates the film, and its traces can be seen all over later Hitchcock, from Joseph Cotten in *Shadow of a Doubt* (1943) to Robert Walker in *Strangers on a Train* (1951) to James Mason in *North by Northwest*.[45]

While Lorre has a comparatively minor role in *The Man Who Knew Too Much*, he is the dominating force of the film and brings to life a flawed production that Hitchcock himself would later describe as the 'work of a talented amateur'.[46] Though his character is not as tormented or dualistic as Beckert, Abbott is an unusually colourful and charismatic villain. Lorre's arrival in Hollywood was marked by similar performances that would highlight his perceived physical eccentricity and the strange magnetism he possessed. His first roles in America were among his best for Hollywood—before he was essentially relegated to B-movies—but also reflect the same themes found in *M*.

Lorre was given starring roles in two films from German cinema notables: *Mad Love* (1935), directed by Lang collaborator and influential cinematographer Karl Freund, and *Crime and Punishment* (1935), helmed by the great Josef von Sternberg. In *Mad Love*, an adaptation of *The Hands of Orlac*, Lorre is as much of a focal point as in *M*; his character is a deranged surgeon driven to violence by sexual obsession and unrequited love, cementing his destiny as an antihero. *Crime and Punishment* is one of Sternberg's least celebrated films, though it boasts another nuanced, sympathetic performance from Lorre as Dostoyevsky's tormented killer-protagonist.

But in general, and despite these successes, throughout the 1930s Lorre spent the bulk of his time on screen, however implausibly, as the Japanese detective Mr. Moto, starring in eight films from that ongoing series. He was relatively prolific during his early years in Hollywood, despite the fact that he had to combat the American perception of Europeans, particularly Europeans with heavy accents. A reflection of these stereotypes is that he was frequently cast in eccentric roles in spy films, as in Hitchcock's *Secret Agent* (1936), *Crack-Up* (1936) and *Lancer Spy* (1937); these would take over his resume in the '40s, where he often worked alongside British actor Sydney Greenstreet. In addition, he took roles as suspicious foreigners or outright criminals in *Nancy Steele is Missing!*

(1937), *Strange Cargo* (1940), *I Was an Adventuress* (1940) and *Island of Doomed Men* (1940).

*M* did allow Lorre to make his mark on the formation of a uniquely American cinematic movement: film noir. While he is associated with *The Maltese Falcon* (1941) and film noir-adjacent war dramas like *Casablanca* (1942), his involvement goes back to one of the first film noir titles (of the 'classic' period of film noir from 1940 to 1958), 1940's *Stranger on the Third Floor*. An ambitious young journalist (John McGuire) believes he has witnessed a murder, but fingers the wrong man. When he is later accused of murdering his own neighbour (Charles Halton), his girlfriend (Margaret Tallichet) must hunt down a mysterious figure: Lorre's titular stranger on the third floor. This film from RKO Radio Pictures contains elements of the horror and psychological melodrama genres, and is one of the earliest examples to combine many of the elements that would become associated with film noir: a running voice-over from the main character, highly stylised visuals influenced by German expressionism, unlikable characters, moral grey areas, the incorporation of dreams and flashbacks, and odd camera angles. The film's urban landscape is a place of fear, paranoia and oppression.

*M*'s influence seems an obvious one. Lorre apparently acted in *Stranger on the Third Floor* as a favour to RKO—he owed them a few days of work—and only actually appears for a few minutes of screen time with scarcely any dialogue. Regardless, he is the dominating presence of the film. His unnamed stranger is an offshoot of Beckert; he is isolated from the world by the machinery of the city itself and has slipped into madness because of it. Violent and dangerous, he wanders the streets and is unable to resist the impulse to kill, but is a surprisingly sympathetic, even tragic figure.

Lorre would also become associated with the horror genre, appearing in horror films and horror comedies—such as *You'll Find Out* (1940), *The Boogie Man Will Get You* (1942), *Arsenic and Old Lace* (1944) and *The Beast with Five Fingers* (1946)—but would occasionally continue to play these tragic antiheroes, such as a disfigured killer out for revenge in *The Face Behind the Mask* (1941). Perhaps fittingly, he returned to the subject matter for his sole effort as writer and director, *Der Verlorene / The Lost One* (1951), which was obviously influenced by *M*. Lorre also starred in this bleak, melancholic film about the horrors of Nazism, made when he briefly returned to Germany after the war. Lorre plays Dr. Rothe, a physician hired to perform experiments for the Nazis. In a series of flashbacks, he relates how he discovered that his fiancée (Renate Mannhardt) was selling government secrets to the Allies. He murdered her and his Nazi associates helped him cover it up so that it looked like suicide by hanging, rather than strangulation. He becomes increasingly paranoid thanks to overwork, depression and the oppressive attentions of his landlady, who is also his dead fiancée's mother (Johanna Hofer); and as a result, is driven to commit more murders.

Though the film is obsessed with death, wartime destruction and decay, Lorre doesn't overtly depict Nazism—as Lang does not in *M*. There are plenty of veiled references to the war, such as air raid sirens, a refugee camp, medical experimentation and bombings. The evils of Nazi bureaucracy are shown in a scene where a fellow scientist and a Nazi leader help Rothe cover up his fiancée's murder and joke about her alleged suicide. Set in Hamburg, the city is a hellish, foreboding place, with the shadowy cinematography clearly influenced by German expressionism. Lorre uses a complex and somewhat confusing narrative structure that builds the sense of dread and paranoia through flashbacks and disturbed memories. Is this Rothe's paranoid fantasy or a violent reality? Like *M*, much of the film's plot is partially based on a real-life crime. Though it was influenced by Guy de Maupassant's 'The Horla,' *The Lost One* was also inspired by a news story about a Hamburg doctor who murdered his assistant and committed suicide. Coincidentally or not, much of Lorre's career can be read as a narrative of the war years and it's easy to draw a line between *M*'s Beckert—a man driven to violence and madness by urban paranoia and mob brutality—to *The Lost One*'s more mature and experienced Dr. Rothe, whose violence is quieter, methodical, state approved, and which turns inevitably upon himself.

**FOOTNOTES**

28. Dawn B. Sova, *Critical Companion to Edgar Allan Poe: A Literary Reference to His Life and Work*. Facts on File, 2001. p. 174.
29. Brian Duffy, 'From a Good Firm Knot to a Mess of Loose Ends: Identity and Solution in Martin Amis' *Night Train*.' *Investigating Identities: Questions of Identity in Contemporary International Crime Fiction*. Ed. Marieke Krajenbrink, Kate M. Quinn. Rodopi, 2009. p. 316.
30. Donald Spoto, *The Dark Side of Genius: The Life of Alfred Hitchcock*. Da Capo Press, 1999. p. 91.

31. Francois Truffaut, *Hitchcock/Truffaut*. Simon & Schuster, 1985. P. 43.
32. Philip Kemp, '*The Lodger: A Story of the London Fog*: The First True Hitchcock Movie.' https://www.criterion.com/current/posts/4688-the-lodger-a-story-of-the-london-fog-the-first-true-hitchcock-movie.
33. Lesley Brill, 'Hitchcock's The Lodger.' *A Hitchcock Reader*. Ed. Marshall Deutelbaum and Leland Poague. Wiley-Blackwell, 2009. p. 82.
34. Ibid.
35. Ibid., p. 83.
36. Philip Kemp, 'The Lodger: A Story of the London Fog: The First True Hitchcock Movie,' https://www.criterion.com/current/posts/4688-the-lodger-a-story-of-the-london-fog-the-first-true-hitchcock-movie..
37. Richard J. Allen, *Hitchcock's Romantic Irony*. Columbia University Press, 2007. p. 23.
38. Dara Waldron, *Cinema and Evil: Moral Complexities and the Dangerous Film*. Cambridge Scholars Publishing, 2013. p. 51.
39. Ibid.
40. Sarah Thomas, *Peter Lorre, Face Maker: Stardom and Performance Between Hollywood and Europe*. Berghahn Books, 2015. p. 37.
41. Stephen Brockmann, *A Critical History of German Film*. Camden House, 2010. p. 121.
42. Stephen D. Youngkin, *The Lost One: A Life of Peter Lorre*. University Press of Kentucky, 2012. p. 62.
43. Ibid., p. 52.
44. Sarah Thomas (2015), p. 33.
45. Farran Smith Nehme, '*The Man Who Knew Too Much*: Wish You Were Here.' https://www.criterion.com/current/posts/2627-the-man-who-knew-too-much-wish-you-were-here
46. Francois Truffaut, *Hitchcock/Truffaut*. Simon & Schuster, 1985. p. 65.

# Chapter Three: The Vampire of Düsseldorf and the Butcher of Hanover

> After my head has been chopped off, will I still be able to hear, at least for a moment, the sound of my own blood gushing from my neck? That would be the pleasure to end all pleasures. —Peter Kürten[47]

While Lang may have been one of the first directors to depict a serial killer as a type of movie monster, this theme recurred in European fairy tales and folklore over the centuries, well before the term 'serial killer' was officially coined in the 1970s by the FBI's Robert Ressler. Peter Vronsky writes, 'Some may argue that these crimes had always been with us but simply had not been recognized or reported, or were disguised as werewolf and vampire myths.'[48] An early German example of a real-life figure who took on this kind of monstrous reputation was sixteenth-century killer and alleged cannibal Peter Stumpp. Known as the 'Werewolf of Bedburg', Stumpp is a particularly notorious example of this German trend where locals conflated a prolific killer with a type of supernatural monster. Stumpp allegedly practiced black magic, worshipped the Devil, and was having a sexual relationship with his own daughter, all of which was disclosed at his public trial in 1589. Connected to the loose witch trials being held in the area at that time, Stumpp was actually tried for being a werewolf in addition to his crimes.

Notions of monstrosity and serial murder developed beyond vampires and werewolves with the unsolved Jack the Ripper killings in the 1880s. These gory, well-publicised slashings of London prostitutes are generally regarded as a turning point in serial crime—at least in the way it was understood by the public and law enforcement—and there is no denying that this type of sexually motivated killing took off in the late nineteenth and twentieth centuries. Vronsky writes, 'Eighty percent of all known male serial killers in the United States appeared between 1950 and 1995. [...] Between 1960 and 1990, confirmed serial homicides increased by 940 percent.'[49] It can be argued that Lang's depiction of Beckert is well ahead of this curve, particularly in terms of how the public perceived serial crime; M falls at the beginning of a believed 'sex crime panic' in the United States, which also spread to Britain and Europe in varying degrees.

Estelle B. Freedman's seminal essay, '"Uncontrolled Desires": The Response to the Sexual Psychopath, 1920-1960', examines this emerging trend, specifically positing that it followed in the footsteps of Lang's film:

> The American media soon began to cater to a growing popular interest in stories of violent, sexual murders committed by men like 'M'. In 1937 the *New York Times* itself created a new index category, 'Sex Crimes,' to encompass the 143 articles it published on the subject in that year. [...] Between 1935 and 1965, city, state, and federal officials established commissions to investigate sexual crime, passed statutes to transfer authority over sex offenders from courts to psychiatrists, and funded specialized institutions for the treatment of sex offenders.[50]

This led to a number of developments within American law and culture to accommodate this perceived panic. Within decades, capturing and treating psychopaths became an industry in and of itself. It is likely that Lang's accurate portrait of a psychopath helped solidify the changing concept of the term, which is crucial to understanding the modern sex crime epidemic. Freedman writes:

> When it first appeared in Europe in the late nineteenth century, the diagnosis of psychopathy did not refer exclusively either to sexual abnormality or to men. [...] It applied to habitual criminals who had normal mentality but exhibited abnormal social behavior. The German psychiatrist Emil Kraeplin used the term psychopathic personality in his influential 1904 textbook to refer primarily to criminals with unstable personalities, vagabonds, liars, or beggars, although he also listed prostitutes and homosexuals.[51]

Psychopathy was first concerned with the idea of 'feeblemindedness' and general criminality in men, though women were also targeted. The late nineteenth century marked a dramatic change in terms of understanding women's sexuality, particularly women's capability to be sexual creatures outside the bounds of marriage and motherhood. Previously, the term psychopath could also apply to prostitutes, women who had extramarital affairs, succumbed to 'hysteria', and so on.

This concept of psychopathy transformed in tandem with the emergence of serial crime, the development of forensics and advancements in abnormal psychiatry that resulted in the cataloguing of sexual perversions and improvement in criminal justice. Freedman writes: 'The sexualization of the male psychopath occurred during the 1930s, when American criminologists became increasingly interested in sexual abnormality and male sexual crime.'[52] Beckert is an embodiment of this: in particular the male sexual deviant was

> thought to attack children, thus simultaneously threatening sexual innocence, gender roles, and the social order. [...] From the origin of the concept, the psychopath had been perceived as a drifter, an unemployed man who lived beyond the boundaries of familial and social controls.[53]

For Freedman, 'the psychopath could represent the threat of anarchy, of the individual unbound by either social rules or individual conscience'.[54] She cites the sex crime panic of the years just before and after WWII when a string of brutal crimes against women, but primarily children, incited a public panic accelerated by a media that sensationalised these crimes and manipulated common fears. She argues that because of social developments and the changing roles of women, children became the ultimate victims. In a sense, Lang was, perhaps unconsciously, capturing this panic on screen and giving it human form in Beckert. Freedman writes:

> Child molestation, like rape, clearly predated the sex crime panics, but for the first time the sexual victimization of children became a subject of popular concern. The gradual acceptance of female sexual desire helped focus attention on children, for if women now actively sought sexual fulfillment, they were less accessible as symbolic victims, while childhood innocence remained a powerful image. In the film *M*, for example, a real-life rapist of women was transformed into a child murderer, as if rape alone were not enough to horrify the modern audience.[55]

## SERIAL MURDER IN WEIMAR GERMANY

The 'real-life rapist of women' in Freedman's quote refers to Peter Kürten, a killer who is widely cited as being the primary inspiration for Beckert. Vronsky writes,

> Peter Kürten, the 'Vampire of Düsseldorf,' stabbed, strangled, and battered at least nine and maybe as many as thirty victims between 1913 and 1930. Sometimes Kürten's

victims went willingly with him to have sex, during which he would suddenly attack them with a knife. At other times, Kürten ambushed his victims, frequently children, on the streets and in parks.[56]

In *The Encyclopedia of Serial Killers*, Michael Newton describes Kürten as 'the product of a violent, abusive childhood'[57] where his large family was crowded into a tiny room and forced to witness his father's (and later Kürten's) abuse of the female family members. Newton references a number of abusive role models in Kürten's life. He was jailed frequently in his early years and lived 'as a nomadic robber' amongst criminals and prostitutes. Unlike Beckert, his murders involved raping women, while he was also responsible for a series of other crimes including setting fires, poisoning and assault. Notably, some of his victims were prepubescent girls.

While serial killers stereotypically have a particular type of victim and style of killing, Kürten's crimes were relatively indiscriminate, including a range of victims and murder weapons. As a teen, he began with bestiality, rape and the killing of animals, but he soon graduated to murder in 1913 after stints in prison and the army that, according to him, had only fuelled his increasingly perverse fantasies. His first known victim was a nine-year-old girl, who he strangled and mutilated. According to him, he was particularly aroused by the sight and sound of dripping blood, returning to the area of the crime to overhear the grief and horror of the locals, and visiting his victims' graves when possible.

His ongoing crimes were interrupted by further bouts of incarceration, until 1929, when he went on a particularly violent spree that included horrifically mutilating and killing girls and women of all ages, as well as a few men. His mounting crimes included rapes, attempted murders, a few strangulations, and beatings with a hammer. Like his first, his final victim was another child, a five-year-old girl, though he would attempt a few other before his arrest in 1930.

Understandably, many of these details could not make their way on screen in 1931 and survive the censors, but Kürten was more of an inspiration for Beckert than a direct point of reference, and other real-life killers found their way into the script thanks to Lang's tireless and somewhat unprecedented research. There was no shortage of examples to choose from. As Vronsky states, 'Postwar Weimar, Germany, became legendary for its serial killers'.[58] Historian and folklorist Maria Tatar dedicated a whole book to the subject, *Lustmord: Sexual Murder in Weimar Germany*, where she examines how this phenomenon appeared in culture: not just *M*, but the artwork of George Grosz and Otto Dix, novels like Alfred Döblin's *Berlin Alexanderplatz*, and so on. Lang himself said:

> At the time that I had decided on the theme of *M*, a number of serial murderers were on the rampage—Haarmann, Grossmann, Kürten, Denke—and so, naturally enough, I asked myself: What led these people to commit these deeds? … Not a single one of these men was a murderer of children, but at about that time children became the victims of terrible crimes in the city of Breslau, and the perpetrator was never caught.[59]

While Fritz Haarmann—known as the Butcher of Hanover—killed more than twenty boys and young men in the early '20s, he was sometimes called the 'Wolfman' because his preferred method of killing involved tearing out the throats of his victims with his own teeth. At other times, he was referred to in headlines as a butcher or a vampire. Haarmann went undetected for several years, partly because he preyed on transient young men whose absence was less likely to draw attention. These were boys looking for food, lodgings, or work. Haarmann was also a figure that bridged the divide between the criminal underworld and law enforcement: he was a police informant, which allowed him to get away with his relatively open homosexuality and his numerous black market dealings. He took full advantage of the country's profound depression and the chaotic atmosphere. Vronsky writes:

> Although many have suggested that the serial murders in Germany were the result of the total collapse of German society following its defeat in World War I, they overlook the fact that some of the Weimar-era serial killers began killing before the war ended, and most had sex crime records going back to long before the war. It is more likely that the postwar chaos unleashed serial killers who were already predisposed to commit their crimes.[60]

Cannibalism and the black market sale of human flesh disguised as animal meat was also a component to the killings of Carl Großman and Karl Denke, who operated during the early years of the Weimar Republic. The Berlin-based Großman allegedly also attacked and molested children early in his life and his later murders went undetected for years because he sold the flesh as animal meat and disposed of the bones in the river. The number of his victims is unknown, though believed to be more than 20, and he was only apprehended because his neighbours overheard him murdering a woman; police found her corpse in his apartment soon after. Similarly, Denke's number of victims is unknown; more than 40 are suspected, given the amount of human flesh found stored in his house, which he was presumably eating and selling. Both Großman and Denke committed suicide before they could be legally executed, and the presumed poverty, isolation and anonymity of both men are reminiscent of Beckert's life in a squalid tenement.

It's surprising that there aren't more German films from this period that focus on serial murder, as it was obviously looming large in the public consciousness at this time. M responds not only to real killers wandering the streets of German cities and towns, but to the inevitable evolution in criminal justice that occurred as a result. Todd Herzog writes, 'During the Weimar Republic a protracted debate took place over how to modernize the process of criminal investigation. In cases such as that of Peter Kürten, traditional methods of visual investigation seemed to go into crisis.'[61] This is certainly reflected in the film, where the police fail to locate any suspect at all and the more innovative methods of the criminal underworld are triumphant.

According to Herzog, this element of the script also mirrored German society: 'Journals like *Kriminal-Magazin*, criminologists such as Robert Heindl, and popular crime writers such as Curt Elwenspoek began to call for a new method of investigation: a vigilant populace united against a common criminal.'[62] In this sense, Lang borrowed from more than the details of murderers' lives and crimes; he used contemporary investigations as a source for inspiration. For example, the main detective, Lohmann, is based on a real inspector in the Berlin Homicide Division:

> Lang's 'fatty Lohmann,' however, is clearly a stand-in for 'fatty Gennat,' the famous homicide detective assigned to the Kürten case, and even such details as the importance of the color of the murderer's pencil are lifted directly from the case. The program issued to accompany the film's premiere even stressed the link between the Düsseldorf murders and Lang's film, incorporating statements by key figures from the Düsseldorf investigation and reproducing the letters that Kürten had written to the press.[63]

Lang 'set out to make a movie about the worst imaginable crime', though the script morphed from a tale of poison pen letters—a la Henri-Georges Clouzot's later commentary on life under Nazi occupation, *Le corbeau / The Raven* (1943)—into a story of serial child murders.[64] Lang wanted to find out the motivation for such acts, what drives the killer, 'what makes him do what he does, what makes him tick'.[65] Though the script was co-written by Thea von Harbou, Lang apparently stumbled across the central idea for the story in newspapers, which were filled with the exploits of Kürten, Haarmann and other killers. Lang writes:

> I thought it fitting to reflect the rhythm of our times, the objectivity of the age in which we are living, and to make a film based entirely on factual reports. Anyone who makes the effort to closely read the newspaper reports about the major homicide cases of the past few years—e.g., the ghastly double murder of the Fehse siblings in Breslau, the Husmann case, or the case of little Hilde Zäpernick, three crimes that are unsolved to this day—will find a strange similarity of events, circumstances that repeat themselves almost as if natural laws were at work.[66]

*M* serves as a sort of synthesis of these horrible deeds and in lieu of offering a specific psychological motivation for such acts, as later serial killer films often do, the crimes in *M* serve as a warning that anyone, anywhere could be capable of murder. Lang wrote a month after the film's release that he had attempted to create something more than 'the artistic reproduction of events: the responsibility of sounding a warning from real events, of educating, and in this way ultimately having a preventive effect'.[67] Even if this claim was meant to appease censors or critics, he clearly struck a nerve with his depictions of the killer's anonymity and the mob's thirst for violence. He describes 'the grotesqueness of an audience infected with a murder psychosis, on the one hand, and the gruesome monotony with which an unknown murderer, armed with a few candies, an apple, a toy, can spell disaster for any child in the street, any child outside the protection of his family or the authorities'.[68]

By this point, Lang was an expert on the subject. He had done extensive research at police headquarters in Alexanderplatz. Youngkin writes:

> Believing there are no small details, he studied its methods and procedures. Through his discussions with psychiatrists, he got into the heads of the criminally insane. He

Beckert snares a child with the promise of a balloon from a Berlin street vendor.

even claimed to have interviewed several mass murderers and talked with members of the Berlin underground that were looking for Kürten.[69]

The killer, during that period, had not yet been captured by police, adding an air of intensity to the scriptwriting process that may explain the emphasis on Beckert's plight as a hunted man. The public and media, of course, followed Kürten's crimes, arrest and trial with an obsessive zeal, and nearly all the details of the case—including Kürten admitting his grotesque sexual propensities—soon became public knowledge.

### THE SYMPATHETIC KILLER

Lang kept this out of the script, preferring instead to focus on the elements that humanised his killer. Lang said, of Kürten, 'I saw him not as a criminal, not as a corpse in a police mortuary slab but as a man, not as an isolate, a phenomenon, but one of many criminals of this time, as a unit in a disintegrating social system'.[70] What makes *M* so horrifying is this sympathetic depiction of Beckert in relation to his crimes. Though they occur off screen, Lang doesn't shy away from presenting them and frequently reminds the audience that Beckert will kill again. Though I have described *M* as a whydunnit, we never actually learn *why* Beckert kills, only that these impulses govern his entire life and he is unable to resist them. In refusing a simple psychological explanation for Beckert's crimes, Lang doesn't allow us to reduce these actions to 'evil', 'immoral' or 'insane' behaviours.

Lang 'focuses almost consistently on the disturbing effects rather than the causes of the crime'.[71] The source of tension within the film comes not from the conventional arc of a mystery or detective story, but from 'the nervous anxiety aroused by the socially disruptive act of murder'.[72] Lang keeps the killer's *modus operandi* intentionally vague and even gives scant details about the victims themselves—all we know is that they are children—or the actual crimes. Tatar writes: 'Rather than displaying the mutilated corpse of the child, Lang represents the girl's death as a spatial and acoustical absence. The vacant stairwell and empty attic, along with the untouched place setting, are counterpointed by Frau Beckmann's increasingly frantic cries, to which there is no response.'[73]

And while it would have been enough of a source of terror to show a killer and his victims—particularly considering that there were not many serial killer films made before this point—Lang added two twists. First, he presents Beckert as the film's de facto protagonist and, ultimately, a sympathetic figure, someone to be pitied even though, in the ultimate contradiction, he is the worst sort of murderer, preying upon innocent children. A point to which I will return later is the absence of sexualised women in *M*. A number of Weimar films explore the dark, destructive side of female sexuality let loose in the world and it would have been predictable to write Beckert as the killer of beautiful young women, as in *The Lodger*, or even a killer of working-class prostitutes—a character type that appears far more in Weimar cinema than in Hollywood films from this period.

The second complication is that the sense of mounting hysteria within the film is located in the anonymity of the killer; anyone could be guilty. Anthony Carlton Cooke writes that 'the idea of the psychopath as a quasi-invisible, alienated individual',[74] combined with the previous understanding of the psychopath as a 'feebleminded offender' is embodied by Beckert:

> [He] appears childlike, which calls to mind clinical and public explanations for the feebleminded offender's alleged preference for child victims. However, Beckert is not developmentally disabled. Neither does he bear any physical markers such as tics or muscle spasms. Nor does he suffer from delusions or hallucinations. Beckert has personality and sexuality disorders, but he also has a firm hold on reality.[75]

Despite his obviously predatory nature and horrific crimes, there is something helpless about him that makes him sympathetic. Beckert could be seen as a precursor to *Psycho*'s Norman Bates, who is also a mixture of feeble, sympathetic and deadly. Lang is able to make Beckert more likable by providing him with a number of contrasting, violent forces: ruthless underworld criminals, fascistic police and mothers who become obsessed with vengeance. There is an obvious conflict between Beckert, as a killer, and the police, but the criminals are also quick to mark him as not *one of them*, as other, hunted even by other criminals. Schränker, their de facto leader and himself a murderer, 'resists recognizing in Beckert a kindred spirit and insists on branding him as an "outsider," an alien being that must be uprooted and exterminated'.[76] They regard him with a seemingly casual dismissal—claiming they have to catch him because he has the police on alert and is thus bad for business—but this seems to mask a deeper fear.

The most remarkable reversal, however, can be found in the behaviour of the neighbourhood mothers; it is they who shape the outcome of the kangaroo court. Tatar writes:

> It is nothing short of astonishing that Lang succeeds in turning a man who commits 'the most heinous crime' into a sympathetic, if also pathetic, character. [...] By the end of the film, Beckert's pathology takes a back seat to the hysteria of the mothers, who are prepared to rush him and to tear him limb from limb. Lang stages a finale that not only shows the killer escaping the clutches of the mothers and their allies, but which also marks the mothers as guilty.[77]

Lang's own assertion that 'every human mind harbors a latent compulsion to murder'[78] is perhaps most nihilistically hammered home by the bloodthirstiness of the mothers. Prevented from tearing Beckert limb from limb, the final shots are of their depressed, disappointed faces in criminal court, where Beckert is permanently spared their personal vengeance when he is found guilty of the murders.

This is a film in which everyone is equally capable of violence. While Beckert is the only character who commits a crime as egregious as child murder, Lang systematically equalises the other character groups until it is clear that everyone is not only capable of, but is driven towards violence. This has a curiously humanising effect on Beckert, whose character arc runs counter to those found in many contemporary serial killer thrillers, as he becomes increasingly desperate and pathetic—increasingly human. He becomes less monstrous and is essentially transformed from perpetrator into victim. Tatar writes, 'Lang repeatedly emphasized the human side of the killer, the side that makes him a victim and engages our sympathies, leading us to feel relief that we escaped his fate but also understanding the degree to which we are all vulnerable to the same dark impulses'.[79]

The violent responses the other characters have toward Beckert likely has to do with his anonymity and ubiquity, which is a major source of anxiety and horror within the film. Despite the fact that much of *M*'s screen time is spent focusing on Beckert, Lang provides a notable lack of detail about the character or his crimes. This is counter to many contemporary serial killer films, which usually take great pains to elaborately explain a serial killer's psychological motivation for his crimes, as well as his distinct *modus operandi*: how he selects, stalks and kills his victims, and what he does with or to the bodies post-mortem.

With Beckert, we learn only of his preference for children, the fact that he kills them in open, public spaces—such as the park at the beginning of the film—and that he is tormented by his urges and lives in poverty and isolation. There is the suggestion that it doesn't matter who Beckert really is or why he kills, which underlies the communal fear that runs throughout the different levels of Berlin society affected by the murders. Cooke writes that underneath the kangaroo court's sentencing of Beckert

> lies a deeper panic based in the greater fear of Beckert's anonymity. [...] Beckert's absence, his resistance to every effort aimed at identifying him, is his presence. His aura of menace comes from anonymity. [...] Beckert's movements among the public produce an atmosphere in which no one is above suspicion and therefore all persons become possible offenders.[80]

Even though Beckert is eventually labelled a killer—quite literally, by the chalk 'M' stamped on his back—and is then captured and forced to stand trial, first by the kangaroo court and later trial in a court of law, there is the impression that something remains elusive, invisible. Tatar writes: 'The criminals and the police may eventually succeed in identifying the murderer, but neither ever penetrates the mystery of the crime, which seems to remain as vaguely formulated in the end as Lang's reference to "some perverted urge".'[81] This lack of explanation for the crimes reflects the absence of true resolution in the film's narrative, which is reminiscent of some of the earlier German expressionist horror films, like *The Cabinet of Dr. Caligari* or *Nosferatu*. In those films, particularly in *Nosferatu*, we never learn the origins of the monster. Though he is vanquished and destroyed thanks to the sacrifice of a young woman, the sense of dread and unease never dissipates from Murnau's film.

## UNCANNY VIOLENCE AND MADNESS IN EXPRESSIONIST CINEMA

In terms of violence and horror during this period in Germany, it's worth addressing one final subject: the aftermath of the Great War. Many of the early German expressionist films, such as *The Cabinet of Dr. Caligari* and *The Hands of Orlac*, are interpreted by modern critics as being direct responses to World War I. Over a decade after the war ended, in 1930 and 1931, Germany was still suffering the repercussions: political instability, economic depression and a society wracked by mass casualties and thousands of young veterans with no obvious prospects. Millions of men were dead, wounded, or traumatised. As such, Weimar cinema is transfixed with ideas of fragile, shattered masculinity and the ghosts of the fallen WWI dead haunting the living. These themes became popular tropes in German literature and cinema and many expressionist films can be read as an attempt to deal with the trauma of war.

This is the main thesis of Anton Kaes's *Shell Shock Cinema: Weimar Culture and the Wounds of War* (2011). He writes, 'the classical cinema of Weimar Germany is haunted by the memory of a war whose traumatic outcome was never officially acknowledged, let alone accepted'.[82] While few of these films directly reference the war, themes of widespread slaughter, trauma-induced psychosis and the constant threat of fatal violence are ever present. The war caused a shock throughout German culture, both for civilians and soldiers, as it 'confronted the living with the long-suppressed reality of violent death'.[83]

Kaes argues that German expressionist films are overwhelmed by themes of violence, murder and horror as a direct result of the war:

> These films translate military aggression and defeat into domestic tableaux of crime and horror. [...] These films feature pathological serial killers, mad scientists, and

naïve young men traumatized by encounters with violence and death. They show protagonists recovering from unspeakable events both real and imagined, and they document distressed communities in a state of shock.[84]

Beckert is a perpetrator of such violence, but also seems to suffer from an unspoken trauma and later in the film reveals he is compelled to kill, but also haunted by his victims. Numerous German expressionist films make reference to characters being haunted by ghosts. Though *M* might not seem like it fits neatly in with German expressionist cinema, which I began to discuss in chapter one, there are many connections between it, *The Cabinet of Dr. Caligari* and *The Testament of Dr. Mabuse*. This notion of being tormented by the dead, even driven mad by them, appears in all three films. Kaes writes:

> In the mass killing of World War I, tens of thousands of war dead were never properly buried and mourned. Corpses were strewn over the battlefields or dumped into mass graves; the trenches themselves often served as graves where soldiers were buried alive after a shell explosion. Hence, there was a widespread fear that the ghosts of unburied soldiers would roam the earth in search of a final resting place. A large spiritist and occultist movement sprang up in Germany in the immediate postwar years because it held out the promise of contact with the spirits of relatives killed in battle.[85]

The three films also share a connection between madness, violence and hypnotism, a nefarious tool for both Caligari and Mabuse, which is also suggested in *M*. It is implied in Beckert's staring into mirrors, and particularly in the scene where he looks into the toy shop window at the swirling spirals. This visual cue suggests a latent madness that will emerge more fully as the film progresses. This theme of madness was also a constant in German society in the interwar years. Kaes writes:

> Throughout the period of the Weimar Republic, autobiographies and confessions of war resisters and war neurotics appeared, recounting how soldiers rebelled against the war by feigning madness, and how they used madhouses as hiding places in which to avoid the real madness of the front.[86]

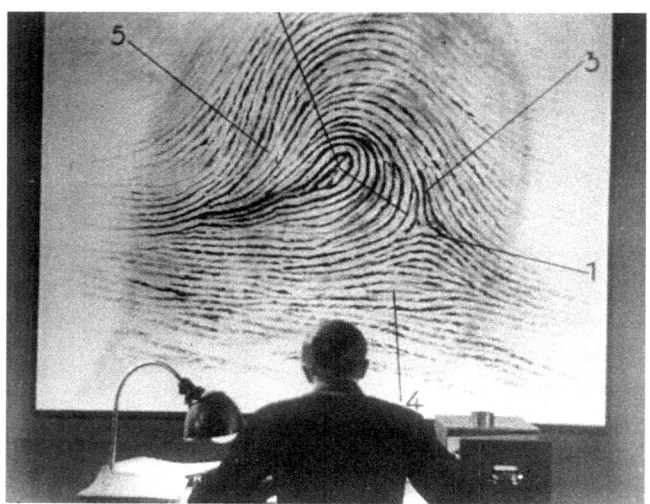

In *M*, the visual trope of swirls and spirals even find their way into forensic evidence.

German expressionist films abound with the theme of protagonists driven to madness and violence by a compulsion; in the case of *The Cabinet of Dr. Caligari*, the compulsion is implanted in Cesare when Caligari hypnotises him. Similarly, Mabuse hypnotises his victims and compels them to commit a variety of crimes: cheating at cards, suicide, theft, and so on. Three of these films' central characters, Cesare, Mabuse and Beckert, are driven by madness and violence until they are pursued by angry mobs eager for justice. Cesare flees across the rooftops of the village, while Mabuse and Beckert are hunted through the bowels of Berlin. But while Mabuse is pursued by law enforcement, Beckert is tracked and captured by the criminal underworld, implying a sort of reversal. Both are tormented by the ghosts of their victims, which Lang seems to suggest is a more absolute punishment than any sort of human justice.

Beckert bears far more in common with Cesare and Mabuse than he does with the few other expressionist characters based on real life killers, namely the few iterations of Jack the Ripper. For example, in Paul Leni's previously mentioned anthology film, *Waxworks*, a young poet (William Dieterle) is hired to write stories for several horrifying figures in a wax museum. One key figure is Jack the Ripper; though utterly unlike Beckert, he appears less as a human form and more as the embodiment of a nightmare—and at the end of his tale, it is revealed the poet has dreamed the whole sequence.

Lotte Eisner calls this 'the most Expressionistic episode' of Leni's film, 'a chaos of forms'.[87] She writes: 'Through the turmoil of this setting glides the phantom of Jack the Ripper (Werner Krauss), elusive, insubstantial. Like the surrounding space the ground is without limits, it dissolves under foot, cracks, congeals, becomes unreal.'[88] In the *Waxworks* segment, Jack does little more than chase the poet and a young woman (Olga Belajeff) through the dark, angular hallways of the museum. In general, the film is more concerned with the horrors of political power—other villains include Ivan the Terrible (Conrad Veidt, yet again)—though the Jack the Ripper sequence is most notable for its stark visual power.

Jack the Ripper is a similarly vague, shadowy figure in G.W. Pabst's *Die Büchse der Pandora / Pandora's Box* (1929), an adaptation of Frank Wedekind's 1904 play, which was one of the first fictional works to reference the London serial killer. In Pabst's film, Lulu (Louise Brooks) makes her way through a series of lovers, causing violence and chaos at every turn thanks to her selfishness and unbridled sexual appetite. In a seemingly inevitable and ironically fitting conclusion, she finds herself alone and destitute in London, where she is forced to turn to prostitution to survive. Her first client is Jack the Ripper (Gustav Diessl), who ultimately murders her. She is inexplicably kind to him and the two have a genuinely romantic moment—she offers to have sex with him for free and he even discards his knife before entering her room—but his impulses win out in the end.

Similarly to *M*, the killer's identity is revealed to the audience through a silhouette in the fog and a wanted poster warning London women. But unlike Beckert, Pabst's Jack the Ripper is a murderer with sex appeal and an appetite for women. He could be read as divine punishment for Lulu's sin of sexual excess, and arrives out of the London fog like a tragic *deus ex machina*. Margaret McCarthy writes: 'Her spilled blood again signals not only just deserts but also the concrete means through which her powers are siphoned off and transplanted into a more acceptable vessel—a male Lustmörder, a murderer of passion, in the form of Jack the Ripper.'[89] Both Leni and Pabst's Ripper characters are symbolic of the horror of sexual excess in a time where women's roles within German society—and the Western world in general—were radically, uncomfortably changing. Beckert, however, lacks the undercurrent of conservative moralising connecting to these other serial killer characters. He is something eerier and more disturbing.

In his 1916 essay 'The Uncanny' Freud wrote of a particular type of terror, which is situated between the familiar and the unfamiliar. The uncanny is not quite the fear of the unknown, but has more to do with recognising something unfamiliar *within* what is familiar to us: a sense of ambiguity and uncertainty. Doubles are crucial to his discussion—also a major component of German expressionist cinema, as I have noted—because they serve to confuse the self:

> The one possesses knowledge, feeling and experience in common with the other, identifies himself with another person, so that his self becomes confounded, or the foreign self is substituted for his own—in other words, by doubling, dividing and interchanging the self. And finally there is the constant recurrence of similar situations, a same face, or character-trait, or twist of fortune, or a same crime, or even a same name recurring throughout several consecutive generations.[90]

This sense of a loss of self is a constant theme throughout German expressionist cinema, particularly in films like *The Cabinet of Dr. Caligari* and *The Hands of Orlac*, and is something Lang explored repeatedly in the early years of his career. *Metropolis* is concerned with the mechanised double of the film's heroine, while *The Testament of Dr. Mabuse* focuses on the titular villain driving others mad in his various criminal pursuits. Much of the doubling that occurs in German expressionist cinema is an example of what Freud refers to as the double becoming 'the ghastly harbinger of death'.[91] He writes of 'the connections the "double" has with reflections in mirrors, with shadows, guardian spirits, with the belief in the soul and the fear of death'.[92]

Though *M* is not as overtly concerned with Gothic themes as many of the other German expressionist horror films, and lacks an obviously supernatural monster, Lang still explores similar themes in his use of a serial killer character. For Freud, the uncanny is represented by what appears to be human, but is not: dolls, mannequins and automata, but also mirror images, shadows, severed limbs, corpses, ghosts and the reanimation of the dead. Beckert is disturbed by his own reflection; his monstrous presence is revealed by shadow and an absence of obvious human form. In the style of

Caligari and Mabuse, the toys in a shop window seem to hypnotise him and draw some murderous impulse to the surface. His madness is connected to his ability to inspire fear and feelings of uncanny terror.

Freud writes, 'We also call a living person uncanny, usually when we ascribe evil motives to him'.[93] Though German expressionism does feature vampires, stone monsters come to life as in *The Golem*, and devils such as in *Faust*, many of the monsters are humans: the homicidal somnambulist and mad psychiatrist of *The Cabinet of Dr. Caligari*, the evil genius of *The Testament of Dr. Mabuse*, the amputee possessed by thoughts of violence in *The Hands of Orlac*. Beckert is an uncanny figure purely because he is a serial killer. He's human, but also something else. His crimes set him apart from society, but Lang dashes any hopes we might have had of seeing him as explicitly other. His anonymity, his very ability to blend in and disappear, reminds us—and the chorus of Berliners in *M*—that anyone could be capable of such acts.

### FOOTNOTES

47. Christopher Berry-Dee, *Cannibal Serial Killers: Profiles of Depraved Flesh-eating Murderers*. Ulysses Press, 2011. p. 175.
48. Peter Vronsky, *Serial Killers: The Method and Madness of Monsters*. Berkley Books, 2004. p. 65.
49. Ibid., p. 19.
50. Estelle B. Freedman, '"Uncontrolled Desires": The Response to the Sexual Psychopath, 1920-1960.' *The Journal of American History*, Vol. 74, No. 1 (June 1987), p. 83.
51. Ibid., p. 87.
52. Ibid., p. 89.
53. Ibid.
54. Ibid., p. 90.
55. Peter Vronsky (2004), p. 101.
56. Michael Newton, *The Encyclopedia of Serial Killers*. Checkmark Books, 2006. p. 69.
57. Ibid., p. 151.
58. Peter Vronsky (2004), p. 68.
59. Fritz Lang, quoted in Maria Tatar, *Lustmord: Sexual Murder in Weimar Germany*. Princeton University Press, 1997. p. 154.
60. Peter Vronsky (2004), p. 70.
61. Todd Herzog, 'Fritz Lang's *M* (1931): An Open Case.' *Weimar Cinema: An Essential Guide to Classic Films of the Era*. Ed. Noah Isenberg. Columbia University Press, 2009. p. 793.

62. Ibid., p. 794.
63. Ibid., p. 775.
64. Maria Tatar (1997), p. 153.
65. Fritz Lang, quoted in Stephen Youngkin (2010), p. 53.
66. Fritz Lang. https://www.criterion.com/current/posts/1457-my-film-m-a-factual-report.
67. Ibid.
68. Ibid.
69. Stephen Youngkin (2010), pp. 53-54.
70. Ibid., p. 54.
71. Maria Tatar (1997), p. 154.
72. Ibid.
73. Ibid., p. 155.
74. Anthony Carlton Cooke, Moral Panics, Mental Illness Stigma, and the Deinstitutionalization Movement in American Popular Culture. Palgrave Macmillan, 2017. p. 24.
75. Ibid.
76. Maria Tatar (1997), p. 168.
77. Ibid., p. 164.
78. Ibid., p. 168.
79. Ibid.
80. Anthony Carlton Cooke (2017), p. 25.
81. Maria Tatar (1997), p. 154.
82. Anton Kaes, *Shell Shock Cinema: Weimar Culture and the Wounds of War*. Princeton University Press, 2011. p. 2.
83. Ibid., p. 97.
84. Ibid., p. 3.
85. Ibid., p. 102.
86. Ibid., p. 73.
87. Lotte Eisner (1973), p. 122.
88. Ibid.
89. Margaret McCarthy, Todd Herzog, 'Surface Sheen and Charged Bodies: Louise Brooks as Lulu in *Pandora's Box* (1929).' *Weimar Cinema: An Essential Guide to Classic Films of the Era*. Ed. Noah Isenberg. Columbia University Press, 2009. p. 576.
90. Sigmund Freud, 'The Uncanny.' 1919. http://web.mit.edu/allanmc/www/freud1.pdf
91. Ibid., p. 9.
92. Ibid.
93. Ibid., p. 13.

# Chapter Four: While the City Sleeps

> Nevertheless, though civilization may have tamed us and curbed our destructive desires in the interests of society at large, there is enough in most of us of the wild, uninhaibited creature to identify ourselves momentarily with the outlaw who defies society and exults in cruelty. The desire to hurt, the desire to kill [...] is closely joined to the sexual urge, under whose dictate no man acts reasonably. —Fritz Lang[94]

As Lang's first sound production, *M* must be carefully examined both in terms of its use of the technology—and how Lang and his production team dealt with this new challenge—and in terms of its depiction of the city. Lang did not explore realist urban environments very often in the early years of his career: *Four Around the Woman* touches upon this, and while *Dr. Mabuse the Gambler*, *Metropolis* and *Spies* are all based in the city, they are also heavily influenced by dystopian science fiction or fantastical descents into the criminal underworld. *M*, on the other hand, was loosely based on actual events and real people, and Lang actually incorporated Berliners as extras in his film.

This allegedly blind beggar and his dog seems to have been inspired by an Otto Dix painting, 'Blind Beggar.'

Despite its convincing set pieces and documentary elements, *M* was not shot on the Berlin streets, but was made over a period of six weeks at the massive Staaken Studios, just outside Berlin, where Lang previously filmed *Metropolis*. A converted zeppelin hangar, it was apparently the largest film studio in the world in the 1920s. There is a rumour that Lang almost wasn't allowed to film at Staaken, because the Nazis assumed the film's original title, *A Murderer Among Us*, was a reference to them and blacklisted him until he cleared up the confusion. According to recent scholarship, this is likely another facet of Lang's own anti-Nazi mythmaking and the title was changed to avoid competing with other, similarly titled films.[95]

Not made for the legendary Ufa studio, *M* was instead a Nero-Film production, a more artistically adventurous studio formed in 1925 by Seymour Nebenzal (cousin of Robert Siodmak) and director Richard Oswald. *M* was also produced by Nebenzal, who worked with everyone from Pabst to Douglas Sirk and was yet another figure important to German cinema driven to exile in Hollywood by the Nazis. He would go on to produce Joseph Losey's *M* (1951) remake there. For Nero-Film, Nebenzal produced a number of films influential in their depiction of Berlin or other urban environments, such as *Pandora's Box*, *Threepenny Opera* and *People on Sunday* (1930). He and Lang would work together again on *The Testament of Dr. Mabuse*.

Nebenzal also worked on some of the innovative early sound films, such as *Threepenny Opera*, though there are few films quite like *M* in these early years of sound cinema. Though the first feature-length 'talkie' was Alan Crosland's *The Jazz Singer* (1927), an American musical, German technicians had worked on developing sound recording capabilities and the first European sound film was the German title *Ich küsse Ihre Hand, Madame / I Kiss Your Hand, Madame* (1929), starring Marlene Dietrich. Perhaps coincidentally, other notable, early European sound films share a number of thematic elements with *M*: Josef von Sternberg's *Der blaue Engel / The Blue Angel* (1930), *Threepenny Opera* and Phil Jutzi's *Berlin-Alexanderplatz* (1931).

Lang was apparently urged by the studio to incorporate sound earlier, in *Woman in the Moon*, but refused, and—as was his fashion—developed the soundscape of *M* in his own particular way. Eisner writes: 'Lang, immediately impressed by the expressive possibilities of sound, very naturally turned his hand to contrasts between sound and image.'[96] I've already discussed that Lang was among the first to borrow the concept of a *leitmotif* from opera and incorporate it into *M*, through Beckert whistling Grieg's 'In the Hall of the Mountain King'; not by Lorre, who apparently revealed after the production began that he couldn't whistle, but by Lang himself.

The score also involved stretches of suspenseful silence—and in that way, the film can be explored as a transitional moment from silent to sound cinema—as well as noise from the street, and various sounds and dialogue to cue action within the film. In a crucial way, sound helped shape the narrative itself and contributed to the mounting sense of suspense throughout the film. Eisner writes:

> Gradually, sound leads to the murderer's discovery. It starts with the oppressed breathing of the hunted monster in the silence of the attics. When the night-watchmen locks the door Lorre's knife snaps in his attempt to force the lock. Then the repeated blows he gives to straighten a nail he has torn from the wall betray his presence.[97]

Through the *leitmotif* and these sequences, Beckert becomes associated with sound, and sound becomes associated with horror. While later horror films certainly make use of contrasting moments of silence with dread-inducing sound, Lang was among the first to explore how the medium could be used to heighten sensations of terror. According to Weimar cinema historian Siegfried Kracauer: 'Lang's imaginative use of sound to intensify dread and terror is unparalleled in the history of the talkies.'[98]

Lang balanced this stylised, specific use of sound with a visual style that borrowed from both German expressionism and a realist, documentary approach. To achieve this balance between such dramatic visual and sound palettes, Lang used a number of talented collaborators he had worked with previously, all of whom had experience on expressionist horror films. The two great cinematographers of Weimar Germany are generally considered to be Karl Freund—who Lang collaborated with on *Metropolis*—and Fritz Arno Wagner, responsible for the cinematography on *M*. Wagner helped shape German horror cinema, including Murnau's *Schloß Vogelöd* (*The Haunted Castle*, 1921) and *Nosferatu*, and he also shot the other major urban film from 1931, Pabst's *Threepenny Opera*. He had collaborated with Lang previously on *Destiny* and *Spies*, and would continue on to *The Testament of Dr. Mabuse*, so it's likely no coincidence that these latter two films and *M* bear a similarly distinctive urban style. The chiaroscuro lighting so indicative of expressionist cinema—which Wagner helped innovate—is used to great effect and often quite unexpectedly throughout *M*.

Wagner's cinematography is far more reliant on documentary-like sequences than the dystopian science fiction look of Freund's work for *Metropolis*, for example. Eisner writes:

> The documentary element that is of decisive importance in this film is achieved not by shooting in actual streets. The camerawork itself is designed to produce the impression that newsreel material has been used—in the shots of the police raids in the allotment gardens; even in scenes where the pictorial composition is emphasized—the singing children and the old organ grinder, or the street where the murderer is confronted by the gang of beggars, filmed from above.[99]

The film's distinctive editing (and sound editing) was provided by Paul Falkenberg, who also worked with Pabst on *Pandora's Box*. Soon after *M*, he would go on to do sound editing for Carl Theodor Dreyer's expressionist horror film *Vampyr* (1932). Art direction was provided by two regular Lang collaborators, Emil Hasler and Karl Vollbrecht, who also worked on *Dr. Mabuse the Gambler*, *Die Nibelungen*, *Metropolis*, *Spies*, *Woman on the Moon* and *The Testament of Dr. Mabuse*. Eisner writes: 'Emil Hesler, Lang's designer here, does not seek effects of light and shade; his cool, precise manner makes for the realism which Lang required.'[100] Though uncredited, director Edgar G. Ulmer would provide set design on the film; he got his start co-directing *People on Sunday*, but soon fled to Hollywood where he made a number of highly underrated films featuring depraved killers, such as *The Black Cat* (1934), serial killer thriller *Bluebeard* (1944) and grimy film noir classic *Detour* (1945).

## URBAN REALISM AND THE STREET FILM

A common element among *Pandora's Box*, *People on Sunday*, *Threepenny Opera* and *M* is the apparently realistic mise-en-scène. These films focus on a combination of 'real' Berliners, such as working-class people or the criminal underworld. *People on Sunday*, directed by Siomak and Ulmer, relates the story of various people around Berlin and declared itself a 'film without actors', casting novices in all the roles. *Pandora's Box* and *Threepenny Opera* include extras cast as prostitutes, criminals and beggars. For *M*, with its focus on working class families, police, criminals, beggars and bar patrons in various scenes, Lang apparently included real criminals among the film's sizeable number of extras, roughly two dozen of whom were allegedly arrested during production.[101] In this way, Lang uses Berlin—and his urban set pieces—in a proto-neorealist sense.

As I have already discussed, Lang used a number of factual elements in his film, such as the details of serial murderers' crimes and psychiatric reports. He also based details of the beggars' lives on real occurrences in Berlin, such as the exchange 'based on a sandwich currency, [which] really did exist in Berlin'.[102] He also frequently consulted with the police:

> He sought advice from the criminal police at the Alex (the nickname given to Berlin police headquarters, at the Alexanderplatz) and was told about their techniques of investigation, and given access to the department's records and memoranda. He talked also to psychiatrists and psychoanalysts, and, not least, to the characters from the 'milieu,' some of whom he later used as extras in the film, notably for the scene of the gangsters' court.[103]

Thus, the city made its way into the film: not the glamorised capital of arts and culture, as Berlin was known in the Golden Twenties, but the grit and grime of the city's real working-class population, where poverty and despair were ever-present. In the 1920s, thanks to the Greater Berlin Act, the city became one of the largest in the world. This new law expanded central Berlin to include a number of surrounding towns and communities, doubling the population to roughly four million people. To accommodate this, the city was rapidly industrialised, with major advancement made in infrastructure and architecture.

Of course, there was a dark side to all this growth. Thanks to inflation and poverty, working class families were unable to keep apace with the booming new housing market and were driven into tenements. Street violence was a new norm, thanks to constant clashes between the left and the right, particularly with the growth of the Nazi party. As unemployment surged, so did crime, including theft, the drug trade and a booming black market. The nebulous underworld took on more structure with the formation of dozens of gangs and organised crime syndicates. A public curiosity about the city's crime problem manifested itself in cinema, but also in the hundreds of crime-themed novels and true crime magazines.

The intersection between crime and culture could be found in the massive network of bars, nightclubs, music venues and brothels for seemingly every taste. The city was especially known for its sexual freedoms and debauched nightlife; it attracted visitors like the young British writers W. H. Auden and Christopher Isherwood. Forced to conceal their homosexuality at home in England, they were able to freely explore it in 1920s Berlin. Isherwood's impressions of the city made it into his short fiction that later inspired the musical *Cabaret*. Both the 1966 stage version from John Kander, Fred Ebb and Joe Masteroff and the 1972 Bob Fosse film are set in 1931 and capture what is often remembered as the urban ethos of Weimar: sexual excess, nihilism and seedy nightclubs. The city's reputation for sexual permissiveness, including wider acceptance of homosexuality, also meant there was a dramatic rise in prostitution, as starving women (as well as teenagers and some men) struggled to feed themselves and their families. This bleak atmosphere frames *M*. As Eisner writes: 'The film ends as it began: with the misery of the backyard amid the dustbins where children have to play in the dreariness and hopelessness of working-class life.'[104]

There is the sense that the Berlin of *M* is somehow responsible for madness, moral evil and the very existence of a monster like Beckert—particularly when reading the city as a product of modernity. A lesser-used secondary title for the film, *A City Searches for a Murderer*, gives Berlin narrative prominence. According to Tom Gunning, 'The city in *M* seems to possess a will of its own; as this secondary title suggests, it could be seen as the protagonist of the film'.[105] As in many of Lang's later films, technology and the development of consumer culture, particularly within urban spaces, becomes ambiguous at best, malevolent at worst. This is particularly evident in *Dr. Mabuse the Gambler*, *Metropolis*, *M* and *The Testament of Dr. Mabuse*. Gunning writes: 'Lang portrays in *M* a systematic understanding of space and order, precisely the sort of modern space described by Henri Lefebvre, abstracted and subordinated to the needs of power.'[106]

As I've discussed, the late 1920s and early '30s was a time of upheaval in German society, when the country was shaken by political instability and new freedoms also resulted in new anxieties. Berlin had a particular role in this. In his introduction to Joseph Roth's *What I Saw: Reports from Berlin, 1920-1933*, Michael Hofmann writes: 'The Weimar period as a whole was characterized by political violence, assassinations, inflation, unemployment, crisis, and instability. [...] Berlin was both a pendant and totem for Weimar.'[107]

Hoffman also writes, 'Berlin is the metropolis as villain'.[108] Joseph Roth certainly describes it this way when he writes about the intersections engorged with pimps and prostitutes as 'if they had been lampposts, or some other organic outgrowth of the street'.[109] The Austrian writer repeatedly describes the city as a sort of inferno: the homeless are 'grotesque-looking figures, as though hauled from the lower depths of world literature',[110] and the wealth of recent immigrants as

> the grotesque spectacle of a hot room at night, containing sixteen naked homeless people, trying to sweat out the soot and coal smoke of a train journey, gives ride to a positively infernal range of interpretations. A series of illustrations, say, to Dante's journeys in the underworld.[111]

Roth writes: 'Everyone is at odds with everyone else. [...] A catastrophe always seems just around the corner.'[112] *M* captures this sense of impending doom and, for a Weimar-era horror film, is somewhat unusual for its urban setting. In some sense, it can be considered a blend of horror themes and tropes found in the realist dramas of the period. Lotte Eisner discussed Berlin in the context of the dour and nihilistic dramas about city life, and she argues that many of these films are connected to earlier, expressionist examples of horror cinema.

> In German films the street represents the call of Destiny—especially at night, with its deserted, treacherous corners, its thundering traffic, its spluttering gaslights, its electric signs, its car headlights, its asphalt gleaming with rain, the lighted windows of its mysterious houses, and the smile of its painted prostitutes; it is the lure and enticement of all poor devils, who, tired of their dull homes and monotonous lives, are out for adventure and escape.[113]

German expressionism gave way to *Neue Sachlichkeit* (New Objectivity) in the middle of the decade. This loose movement can be seen as an early precursor to neorealism and something of a parallel to poetic realism in France, as it focused on stories about working class people struggling to survive in the city, often with a pessimistic edge. Some of these titles became known as *Straßenfilm*, or the street film, because of their emphasis on gritty stories about life on the streets of Berlin, where the city took on a distinct persona through Weimar culture. Sabine Hake writes:

In the early years of the Weimar Republic the word *Straße* (street) itself began to appear with notable frequency in the titles of books, paintings, poems, and films. While some of the meanings attributed to a jaunt down the avenue in the cultural discourse of the time were based on firsthand experience, others were the fantasies (and nightmares) of individuals for whom the cityscape served as a projection surface for otherwise inexpressible desires and fears, representing all of the promises and concomitant dangers of venturing outside the safe walls of home.[114]

Key titles include Karle Grune's *Die Straße / The Street* (1923), which was one of the first to be categorised as a street film and Pabst's *Die freudlose Gasse / The Joyless Street* (1925). In *The Street*, a man (Anton Edthofer) leaves the comfort of his bourgeois life for an adventure in the city, which quickly transforms into an urban hell where he is beset by criminals and prostitutes. Through the expressionistic visuals, Grune implies that the street itself has a sinister awareness, and his film has a number of the genre hallmarks. Hake writes:

> Made between 1923 and 1930, these urban melodramas most often take place in a contemporary setting and feature a dissatisfied middle-class man who, burning to break out of home and routine, ventures into the city at nightfall, coming face-to-face with the criminal underworld and a dangerous seductress on his way. In many such films the urban avenue is portrayed as a threatening and anxious space, which the protagonist then attempts to escape by returning home to the safe structure of middle-class family life.[115]

Citizens of Berlin huddle together miserably in Pabst's *The Joyless Street*.

In a similar vein is Pabst's *The Joyless Street*, which is considered one of the classics of the genre and included an early role for Greta Garbo. It prominently features one of the main themes of Weimar cinema: destructive sexuality. Like *The Street*, urban nightlife is equally alluring and repulsive. Set in Vienna, *The Joyless Street* follows two women (Asta Nielsen and Garbo) involved with a hotel brothel, who are struggling to survive the economic depression. Unlike many of the Hollywood films from the period, this is not a tale of moral absolutes: even the 'good' characters are forced to debase themselves, while Pabst also gives the film's villains (such as Werner Krauss's butcher) moments of humanity. Hake writes:

> With its thematic emphasis on vision and subjectivity, crime and sexuality, the relationship between private and public life in the city, and the decline of the middle class, *The Joyless Street* stands as one of the major representatives of the Weimar street film.[116]

*The Joyless Street* depicts the lurid exploitation of women, while also focusing on their individual stories with notes of pathos and melodrama. For all intents and purposes, it could be categorized as a woman's film, a loose grouping of movies that included Gothic thrillers, moral dramas, melodrama and outright horror films, all of which feature women as protagonists and are generally set in the home and concern topics like children, families and romantic relationships. But in a far cry from most Hollywood cinema, in *The Joyless Street* women are beaten, murdered, and themselves become murderers. They are forced to trade sex for survival, and become ruthless, immoral.

This is also the general theme of Pabst's previously mentioned *Pandora's Box*, as well as *Tagebuch einer Verlorenen / Diary of a Lost Girl* (1929). Hake writes, 'the attractions of the street film, [...] usually revolve around the spectacle of a simultaneously alluring and threatening sexuality associated with the figure of the prostitute'.[117] Even street films with male protagonists, like Gerhard Lamprecht's *Die Verrufenen / Slums of Berlin* (1925) or *Berlin-Alexanderplatz*, both based on the works of prominent novelists Heinrich Zille and Alfred Döblin, feature prostitutes in major roles. In both of these films, sympathetic prostitute characters attempt to rescue a defenceless, destitute man struggling to reenter the world—and return to the street—after a prison sentence.

And while *M* details a similar, bleak struggle of families in the tenements, it is quite a different beast, because it lacks the intersection between sexuality and criminality— primarily because of the absence of prostitute characters. Instead, Beckert's sexual impulses are not directed at prostitutes, but at children. Unlike in the street film, women are not sexual beings in *M*; they are either middle-aged mothers, wracked with grief and obsessed with vengeance, or children, being led, by Beckert, like lambs to the slaughter. The erotic nightmare of many street films becomes a vision of nihilistic horror. Tom Gunning writes that *M* offers 'the image of city inhabitants as isolated, atomised individuals under a regime of terror. [...] the private face of living under fascism as the nightmare of modernity'.[118]

## CRISES OF MASCULINITY AND EMPTY SPACES

A notable connection between the street film and *M* is that both represent a crisis in German masculinity, one that typically leads to violence. This type can be found in a number of expressionist horror films that have complicated depictions of masculinity. *Warning Shadows* explores the fantasies of a jealous husband. *The Cabinet of Dr. Caligari* and *The Hands of Orlac* present a man who is the passive instrument of violence orchestrated by someone else. In *The Golem*, a jealous young man incites the monstrous creature to violence because he witnesses the woman he loves in bed with another man. In *Nosferatu*, a woman has to be the hero and rescue both her husband and their community from a plague-spreading vampire.

But the street film deals with this more subtly. Emil Jannings was an actor who frequently portrayed characters whose primary drama was a crisis of masculinity, most notably in Murnau's *Der letzte Mann / The Last Laugh* (1924). He stars as a once proud hotel doorman who is demoted to janitor when he becomes too old, initiating a steady descent into humiliation and misery. Sabine Hake writes:

> Jannings began to specialize in stories of defeat and humiliation, including the kind of sexual humiliation portrayed in E. A. Dupont's *Varieté* (*Variety*, 1925) and Josef von Sternberg's *Der blaue Engel* (*The Blue Angel*, 1930). In all these films his reenactment of the undoing of the authoritarian subject, the Wilhelminian Untertan, not only expressed historical audiences' deep ambivalence about modernity and modernization but also translated the shock of the new into the gendered and generational terms that connected politics and erotics in highly suggestive and often problematic ways.[119]

Throughout his career, Jannings 'remained closely identified with the underlying crisis of masculinity' and 'he came to stand in for the affective dilemmas of an entire generation confronted with the inherent violence behind the process of modernization'.[120] Though Beckert is more overtly violent than many of Jannings' characters, whose violence is often directed inward, Beckert fits within this type of the emasculated, humiliated man. His perverse sexual attraction to children, his small physical stature, and seemingly timid nature are all symbolic of this, as is his transformation from murderer to victim throughout the film. Like Jannings' character, the porter, in *The Last Laugh*, Beckert is a citizen of the Berlin tenements, a cinematic space generally 'ruled by housewives and children'.[121]

Location is of prime importance to many street films, where the city becomes a character in and of itself—as in *Dr. Mabuse, the Gambler*, *Metropolis* and *M*. The tenement setting helps to define these male characters, as they are essentially isolated in a sea of women and children. Such is the case with *The Last Laugh*, but it's also true of *M*, where very few men are seen in the tenements: all able-bodied men, whether cops, criminals, or regular Joes, are active in other spaces. The tenements are places of crushing poverty and loneliness, representing the dark side of modern urban living. Describing *The Last Laugh*, Hake writes: 'The porter's apartment, the staircase, and the narrow inner courtyard are dark and confining spaces, reminiscent both of the oppressive familiarity explored by the chamber-play dramas and the unhealthy living conditions.'[122]

Underlining the importance of urban locations to M, Lang uses a number of different set pieces to evoke different moods: depression and isolation, but also horror. Todd Herzog writes:

> The first half of the film is largely preoccupied with detailing empty spaces: vacant basements, open fields, empty streets. [...] The empty public spaces of the early part of *M* are all, essentially, crime scenes or potential crime scenes.[123]

These isolated urban locations similarly become as forbidding as any Gothic castle, evoking a mood of terror and isolation as effectively as the village set pieces in *The Cabinet of Dr. Caligari* or *The Golem*, or the bleak castle of *Nosferatu*. Absence and lack become quickly associated with horror in *M*, as bodies—particularly bodies associated with violence—are often indicated by their absence: Beckert himself, who first appears in silhouette, the murdered bodies of children, which are suggested by abandoned toys and balloons, but are never directly shown. As Tom Gunning writes, 'the film does pivot around Hans Beckert, but around his absence rather than his presence, around the search for this mysterious and initially elusive figure. [...] He is the film's blind spot, its aporia, rather than its point of coherence.'[124]

Peter Gay refers to Weimar Berlin as 'a paranoid world, filled with enemies: the dehumanizing machines, capitalist materialism, godless rationalism, rootless society, cosmopolitan Jews, and that all-devouring monster, the city'.[125] Lang depicts this quite literally in *Metropolis*, but hints of it can be found as early as *The Wandering Shadow* and *Vier um die Frau*. I would argue that this theme comes to a particularly violent conclusion in *M* and *The Testament of Dr. Mabuse*, where Lang takes the expressionist trappings often relegated to eighteenth-century villages and remote forest settings, and brings them to the city.

Beckert is made monstrous simply because of how Lang and cinematographer Fritz Arno Wagner capture his shadow, which Eisner describes as 'that shadow of doom proclaiming the imminence of a menacing but still unseen character, a shadow which slips across the floor and reaches the person threatened before the real contact occurs'.[126] Even though *M* lacks overt supernatural elements and is set in the grimy, bustling city, Lang is able to evoke a sense of uncanny horror through his use of visual style: primarily shadows and eerie reflections in mirrors, as well as 'cigarette smoke floating in the glow of a hanging lamp'.[127] Though villages are beset by literal monsters in *The Golem* and *Nosferatu*, Beckert is arguably more terrifying because he cannot be easily identified as Other, as non-human. He uses the crowded city to blend in to his environment, where, as 'in Romantic literature, one frequently does not know whether a character will eventually prove sympathetic or a wicked demon'.[128]

Something about the anonymity of city life is the source of terror for Beckert's character, which connects back to a fear mined by German expressionism: the lack of individual, specifically male, identity. Eisner writes that, 'This perpetual mirroring on glass of desired objects or persons is found in Fritz Lang's *M* and *The Woman in the Window* (1944) and Pabst's *Die Dreigroschenoper*'.[129] But when Beckert looks at himself in the mirror, he is struck with a particular type of disgust, even terror, that seems to stir his criminal impulses. This also occurs when he looks in the window of a toy shop and spies his faint reflection. As the nineteenth-century German poet Heinrich Heine wrote, 'Nothing can scare us more than chancing to see our face in a glass by moonlight'.[130]

Despite the connection between *M* and the street films, Lang subverts the genre by his presentation of Berlin itself as a site of horror. This is a varied community in the grip of fear and paranoia. They suffer not just from poverty and depression, but from unspeakable violence. Unlike in a more straightforward social drama, Lang's presentation of the tenement community and especially the kangaroo court represents a divided social stratum essentially united by violence. Because of fear, they come together despite their differences, but also because of a desire for violent revenge that becomes more bloodthirsty as the film progresses. There were a number of German films made in the late 1920s and early '30s that incorporate these realist elements and focus on murderers and criminals, but few that encounter mob violence in the same way.

An interesting contrast can be found in another 1931 film, *Emil and the Detectives*, from social realist director Gerhard Lamprecht and with a script from two up and coming filmmakers, Emeric Pressburger and Billy Wilder. A young boy, the titular Emil (Rolf Wenkhaus), travels from his small town to Berlin with money for his grandmother. But on the train, he is given drugged chocolate by a strange man (Fritz Rasp), who steals his money while Emil is unconscious. He teams up with a band of local children, 'the detectives', who help him hunt down the stranger and reclaim his money. While the mob of children subdues him, he is arrested and revealed to be a notorious criminal, and Emil is given a sizeable cash reward.

There are some undeniable parallels between *M* and *Emil and the Detectives*. There is the subtle implication of paedophilia; a man knocking a child unconscious with drugged chocolate certainly has unsavoury undertones and the scene is quite hallucinatory—and allegedly went on to influence a similar sequence in Hitchcock's *The Lady Vanishes*. But even more so, the fact that a seemingly invisible group of people—children in one film, beggars in the other—are used to locate a criminal subverts the traditional formula of police or an independent detective coming up against a mysterious antagonist.

A ubiquitous army of children swarm Berlin in *Emil and the Detectives*.

Many of the crime films from this period explore the impact urban life and economic depression have on crime, where pathological impulses and desperation overlap. A key example is Phil Jutzi's 1931 adaptation of Alfred Döblin's classic novel of crime and murder in poverty-ridden Berlin, *Berlin-Alexanderplatz*, which follows Franz Biberkopf's (Heinrich George) descent into the city's underworld. After he is released from prison, he can't seem to re-enter normal life and a series of unfortunate circumstances send him into a hellish spiral of crime from which there is no salvation.

Films about a tormented killer were obviously popular enough to result in several expressionistic Dostoyevsky adaptations throughout the decade, including Robert Weine's *Raskolnikov* (1923) and Erich Engels and Fedor Ozep's *Der Mörder Dimitri Karamasoff / The Murderer Dmitri Karamazov* (1931). Weine would return to similar themes with *Panik in Chicago / Panic in Chicago* (1931), in which a gangster in Chicago uses a variety of disguises to hide from police and pose as a regular member of society. Like Weine, director Robert Siodmak also regularly explored similar themes in films like *Voruntersuchung / Inquest* (1931), which follows the investigation of a prostitute's murder in a boarding house, or *Der Mann, der seinen Mörder sucht / The Man in Search of His Murderer* (1931), a crime comedy about a man who hires someone to assist with his suicide, but then changes his mind.

In general, though, the urban crime thrillers from this period were more action or mystery-oriented than they were concerned with psychological terror. A slightly earlier example of serial crime can be found in *Der Würger / The Wrecker* (1929), about a man who causes train accidents as a ploy to drive people to the bus service he controls. There are a number of examples of what could be described as proto-film noir that were likely inspired by film serials such as *Fantômas* or Lang's *The Spiders*, for example, *Die Yacht der sieben Sünden / Yacht of the Sevens Sins* (1928), about murder on a ship with a number of likely suspects including a femme fatale, or the somewhat similar *Das Schiff der verlorenen Menschen / The Ship of Lost Men* (1929), a Marlene Dietrich-vehicle directed by Maurice Tourneur.

Gangs of criminals featured increasingly in films later in the 1920s, such as Lupu Pick's *Das Panzergewölbe / The Armored Vault* (1926), *Männer ohne Beruf / Men Without Work* (1929) and early Edgar Wallace adaptation *Der rote Kreis / The Red Circle* (1929).[131] But undeniably the film from the period with the closest relationship to *M*—at least in terms of how the criminal underworld was portrayed—is Pabst's *The Threepenny Opera*, released just a few months earlier. Based on the scathing, socialist play of the same name by Bertolt Brecht and Kurt Weill, Pabst's film follows Mackie Messer (Rudolf Forster), 'Mac the Knife', a powerful criminal in Victorian London who sets his sights on Polly Peachum (Carola Neher), the daughter of a rival gang boss. Her father (Fritz Rasp) is in charge of the network of beggars spread throughout the city, similar to the same organisation within *M*. Mackie is introduced within the first minutes of the film as a monstrous criminal: in the popular song 'Mac the Knife', it's explained that he has stabbed both men and women to death, raped a woman, and sat smiling while a tenement full of children burned to the ground, with the implication that he started the fire.

Like *M*, the ultimate suggestion of *The Threepenny Opera* is that there is little difference between polite society and the criminal underworld. After a series of trials, Mackie becomes a bank director, thanks to the clever interventions of his new wife. Though Pabst's film only loosely reflects Brecht and Weill's musical, leaving out much of the music and some of the bitter satire, both *Threepenny Opera* and *M* share the view that businessmen, police officers, and the seemingly above-board strata of society are, in reality, indistinguishable from murderers, gangs of thieves and the beggars that invisibly wander the streets.

Despite the fact that he is a known, even celebrated murderer, Mackie is able to woo a pretty young woman and convince her, without much ado, to marry him; he is also an apparently respected (or at least feared) member of the community, and more or less steps from a jail cell into his new role as bank director and prominent businessman with ease. This deeply cynical 'happy' ending is the inverse of Beckert's fate in *M*, where Lang's killer is hunted, captured, tried in two courts, and narrowly avoids a violent execution at the hands of local mothers. But despite their different trajectories, both films seem to confirm that crime and violence are inevitable.

## LANG AND CRIME AFTER *M*

Lang's follow up to *M*, *The Testament of Dr. Mabuse*, is similarly concerned with the ubiquity of crime. Nearly a decade after the events of *Dr. Mabuse the Gambler*, Dr. Mabuse (Rudolf Klein-Rogge) has spent years in an insane asylum, where he feverishly writes out detailed crime plots that are secretly being carried out by a local gang. When anyone attempts to reveal this conspiracy, they are silenced, though a police inspector still tries to trace the crimes back to Mabuse. Ultimately Mabuse becomes a disembodied spirit, free to spread evil through the world, unchecked, able to possess men's minds and even their flesh at will. Mabuse is 'kept alive through the technological recordings and transmissions of his voice, delivering his messages while keeping his physical presence hidden, untraceable, and therefore unseizable'.[132] This is a radical advancement of *M*'s thesis that anyone, anywhere is capable of violent crime. The Berlin of *The Testament of Dr. Mabuse* is a place where crime is the rule and law, order and justice are impotent forces.

Tom Gunning calls the film an 'uncanny prefiguring of the Nazi movement',[133] and Lang fled the country not too long after its release. Mabuse's ultimate goal is a world consumed by crime and violence, where reason is always subject to madness. During the film, the spectral Mabuse states, 'When humanity, subjugated by the terror of crime, has been driven insane by fear and horror, and when chaos has become supreme law, then the time will have come for the empire of crime'. As the themes of technology, surveillance and paranoia took hold in *Dr. Mabuse the Gambler*, *Spies* and *M*, here they are at their ultimate expression and the law is powerless against them.

Like *M*, *The Testament of Dr. Mabuse* presents another reimagining of thriller and mystery tropes, taken to the extremes of totalitarian terror. If Beckert's murders are terrifying partly because they could have been committed by anyone, Mabuse's terror is based in the fact that, Caligari-like, he is able to incite anyone to violence through hypnotism, manipulation, or sheer force of will. Erik Butler writes:

> *Testament* parodies the tidy explanations in which detective stories typically culminate. [...] The film unfolds as a series of ingenious maneuvers that draw closer and closer to an adversary who escapes in the end because he is all accident, with no essence. Clues reveal movement in a field of darkness, but the gloom is too thick to allow the figure to be tracked successfully. A series of substitutions and ciphers disrupt and delay the disclosure of the truth indefinitely.[134]

Crime seemed to obsess Lang in that decade. His slightly later American films continued to explore the relationship between criminal justice, mob violence and urban poverty, particularly titles like *Fury* (1936), *You Only Live Once* (1937) and *You and Me* (1938). *Fury* examines similar material as *M*, albeit from a different vantage point. Spencer Tracy stars as a man wrongly accused of murder who is nearly a victim of mob violence. Consumed by anger and bitterness, he fakes his own death in order to punish the perpetrators, but is eventually tormented by his conscious. Anton Kaes writes:

> Lang's film is ultimately less interested in politics than in social and psychological questions, such as the mob's inherent disposition toward violence or the power of the individual. Exiles and immigrants who had fled Fascist Europe for an idealized America felt an innate urgency to warn against mob mentality or the breakdown of law and order. They had seen the fanatical mindlessness of the masses with their own eyes.[135]

While *Fury* can be read as a continuation of the mob violence theme as it was shaped by Lang's own personal experiences in the early days of Nazi Germany and his new life as a refuge, there is a definite connection between Joe, *Fury*'s protagonist, and Beckert. Both men are exiles, hunted and tormented by an entire community. And while Beckert's crimes are indeed horrific and Joe was merely in the wrong place at the wrong time and has been falsely accused, Lang creates many parallels between the two characters. Key scenes in both films include the harried protagonist delivering a monologue while looking directly into the camera. A major theme for both films can be summed up by Kaes: 'The rule of the law itself is no guarantor against base instincts of revenge.'[136]

If there was to be a general thesis taken from both of *You Only Live Once* and *You and Me*, it's that it doesn't seem to matter whether or not someone is genuinely guilty of a crime: they will be treated a particular way based primarily on the perception of guilt. These films, as well as *Dr. Mabuse the Gambler*, *Metropolis* and *The Testament of Dr. Mabuse*, also explore different ways in which the experience of poverty and urban decay directly results in crime. Nick Smedley describes 'Lang's message that society creates its own criminals',[137] which was particularly unpalatable to American audiences:

> The idea that people are poor just because they are lazy or that they commit crimes simply through weakness of character is as outmoded as the doctrine of original sin from which it stems. The way to abolish crime is not to hush up its existence but to examine its sources and, having laid them bare, to eliminate them.[138]

This echoes Lang's own statements that *M* is an attempt to raise awareness about crime in order to prevent it, but the undercurrent of social criticism is hard to ignore. *M*, *The Testament of Dr. Mabuse*, and these early American films can be read as a way to understand how crime and poverty affect communities.

These Lang films also foreshadow later thrillers about murder that flirt with horror genre themes, like Henri-Georges Clouzot's *Le corbeau* or Sidney Gilliat's *Green for Danger* (1946). These cinematic worlds are as similarly bleak and isolating as the Berlin of *M*, but citizens are driven to accuse one another of various crimes, driving them collectively towards acts of hysteria and violence. The vengeance suggested in *M* is carried out in *Le corbeau* in particular, where the mother of a victim cuts the throat of her son's killer. Granted, this film was made in Nazi-occupied France, where Gestapo methods of law and order—just loosely emerging in 1931—were in full sway across Europe.

**FOOTNOTES**

94. Fritz Lang, as quoted in Eisner (1973), *Fritz Lang*, p. 112.
95. For a brief time, Nazis actually applauded the film; for example, in his diary, Joseph Goebbels celebrated the fact that he thought *M* was strongly in favour of the death penalty.
96. Lotte Eisner (1973), p. 320.
97. Ibid., p. 322.

98. Siegfried Kracauer, *From Caligari to Hitler: A Psychological History of the German Film*. Princeton University Press, 2004. p. 220.
99. Lotte Eisner, *Fritz Lang*. De Capo Press, 1986. p. 116.
100. Ibid., p. 116.
101. Paul M. Jensen. *The Cinema of Fritz Lang*. A. S. Barnes & Co., 1969. p. 94.
102. Lotte Eisner (1986), p. 114.
103. Ibid.
104. Ibid., p. 128.
105. Tom Gunning, *The Films of Fritz Lang: Allegories of Vision and Modernity*. British Film Institute, 2000. p. 164.
106. Ibid., p. 180.
107. Michael Hofmann, Introduction. *What I Saw: Reports from Berlin, 1920-1933*, by Joseph Roth. W.W. Norton & Company, 2004. p. 12.
108. Ibid., p. 17.
109. Joseph Roth, *What I Saw: Reports from Berlin, 1920-1933*. W.W. Norton & Company, 2004. p. 53.
110. Ibid., p. 65.
111. Ibid., p. 70.
112. Ibid., p. 102.
113. Lotte Eisner (1973), p. 251.
114. Sabine Hake, 'Who Gets the Last Laugh? Old Age and Generational Change in F.W. Murnau's *The Last Laugh* (1924).' *An Essential Guide to Classic Films of the Era*. Ed. Noah Isenberg. Columbia University Press, 2009. p. 363.
115. Ibid., p. 393.
116. Ibid.
117. Ibid., p. 341.
118. Tom Gunning (2000), p. 174.
119. Sabine Hake (2009), p. 313.
120. Ibid., p. 319.
121. Ibid., p. 350.
122. Ibid.
123. Todd Herzog (2009), pp. 796-797.
124. Tom Gunning (2000), p. 164.
125. Peter Gay, *Weimar Culture: The Insider as Outsider*. W.W. Norton & Company, 2001. p. 96.
126. Lotte Eisner (1973), p. 133.
127. Ibid., p. 200.
128. Ibid., p. 106.
129. Ibid., p. 252.

130. Ibid., p.129.
131. British writer Edgar Wallace's novels would later serve as inspiration for a series of colourful, often lurid crime/horror films in the postwar years, which in turn inspired the Italian *giallo* films.
132. Tom Gunning, '*The Testament of Dr. Mabuse*.' https://www.criterion.com/current/posts/603-the-testament-of-dr-mabuse
133. Ibid.
134. Erik Butler, 'Dr. Mabuse: Terror and Deception of the Image.' *The German Quarterly*, Vol. 78, No. 4, Focus on Film (Fall, 2005). p. 488.
135. Anton Kaes, 'A Stranger in the House: Fritz Lang's "Fury" and the Cinema of Exile.' *New German Critique*, No. 89, Film and Exile (Spring - Summer, 2003), p. 36.
136. Ibid., p. 47.
137. Nick Smedley, 'Fritz Lang's Trilogy: The Rise and Fall of a European Social Commentator.' *Film History*, Vol. 5, No. 1 (Mar. 1993), p. 12.
138. Ibid., p. 2.

## Chapter Five: The Pleasure to End All Pleasures

> It's there all the time, driving me out to wander the streets, following me, silently, but I can feel it there. It's me, pursuing myself! I want to escape, to escape from myself! But it's impossible. I can't escape, I have to obey it. I have to run, run… endless streets. I want to escape, to get away! And I'm pursued by ghosts. Ghosts of mothers and of those children… they never leave me. They are always there… always, always, always! Except… when I do it. —Hans Beckert, *M*

In terms of Lang's unique depiction of serial murder, *M* was widely influential in the two decades following its release and has gone on to shape contemporary genre cinema, particularly in the increasing fascination with serial killers in the films of the 1970s, '80s and '90s. This is partially because Lang was ahead of a wave of understanding of sex crimes in the 1930s-'40s, when the concept came into the public consciousness for the first time. Simultaneously, *M* served as a precursor to film noir—a film movement Lang himself shaped from the inside after his emigration to America—a series of films also concerned with urban terror, criminal compulsion and human darkness.

As *M* reflected the paranoias of a Germany in turmoil, a decade later film noir in America would reflect the horrors of WWII and the Holocaust, the lingering misery of the Great Depression, and fears about the developing Cold War. While film noir is more of a movement than a cohesive genre, the plots of these films reveal the murky underbelly of American life: the failure of the American dream, of industry, masculinity, the family unit and authority. These are worlds plagued with paranoia, corruption and crime, where characters are often isolated and lonely: themes also focal to *M*. A lot of film noir titles—and thrillers that exist on the fringe of the movement—focused on murderers and violent crime. Like Beckert, film noir protagonists were often doomed and lonely men, subject to the cruel whims of fate, a type also regularly exploited by Hitchcock through his recurring 'wrong man' trope.

Hollywood reflected the fact that the US was plagued with an increasing number of sexually-motivated murderers, a subject that inevitably found its way from the front page of the newspaper into movie theatres, as in *M*. While 'serial killer' was not a term used in wartime America, the concept of a sexually deviant murderer was becoming popularised by the media and true crime details began to appear in the literature and cinema of the period. Beginning in the 1930s, these types of crimes were on the rise. Examples abound. In 1930, career criminal, rapist (he claimed to have raped 1,000 men and women) and murderer Carl Panzram was executed. 'Lonely Hearts' killer Harry F. Powers was executed in 1932 after murdering two women and three children, and his crimes would go on to be the basis for the 1955 horror-noir film *Night of the Hunter*.

In 1934, the grandfatherly Albert Fish, a child killer, rapist and cannibal, was arrested, later to be executed for his troubles. Joe Ball, a WWI soldier and Texan bootlegger, killed women from 1936 to 1938; he allegedly fed his victims to his pet alligators. The never-identified Cleveland Torso Murderer mutilated and dismembered at least a dozen victims in areas of Ohio and Pennsylvania throughout the 1930s. One of his victims, a headless woman found on the beach of Lake Erie in 1937 but never identified, was nicknamed 'The Lady of the Lake'. This was also the name of a Raymond Chandler novel from 1943 (later adapted to film) about a dead woman found in a lake, incorrectly identified. William Heirens, the 'Lipstick Killer', began stabbing women in 1945 and wrote a note in lipstick on the wall, 'For heaven's sake catch me before I kill more, I cannot control myself'. These crimes were the basis for Lang's 1956 film noir *While the City Sleeps*.

As recent emigres, Hitchcock and Lang were among the first to explore this theme within Hollywood, and it would come to be the overriding obsession of both of their careers, in turn influencing several generations of directors. While serial killer-themed cinema became widely popular with mainstream audiences in the 1970s and '80s, this theme was more of a rarity in the 1940s and '50s. Many of the films released during the postwar years to explore this theme were quite obviously influenced by *M*, particularly in their use of the tormented murderer as protagonist.

In addition to the previously mentioned *Stranger on the Third Floor*, with Lorre as another disturbed killer, one of the earliest examples of a film noir title to explore sexually motivated murder can be found in *I Wake Up Screaming* (1941), where an ambitious young woman is killed as she is on the verge of becoming a star. The menacing detective in charge of the case, Ed Cornell (Laird Cregar), ultimately proves to be psychopathic.

As in *M*, the city is a character in its own right, and this New York is a place of seedy menace and sexual psychosis. The undercurrent of depravity is pervasive throughout the film, as nearly all the male characters are scoundrels, sexually obsessed stalkers or exploiters of women, and at least one of them is a murderer.

Though his career was tragically cut short by his early death, Cregar would go on to appear in similar roles and this typecasting is reminiscent of Lorre's fate. Cregar would star in John Brahm's remake of *The Lodger* (1944), with quite a different interpretation of the novel than Hitchcock's film: the titular lodger is the murderer and Brahm paints quite a disturbing picture of this paranoid, disturbed killer obsessed with cutting women's beauty out of the world. The film has far more in common with *M* than it does with Hitchcock's original. Cregar played a similar character again in *Hangover Square* (1945), a troubled composer who murders women during periods of mental blackout. Like Lorre's Beckert, Cregar was almost always cast as a sympathetic killer, and one who figures as the film's protagonist. In *Hangover Square*, he is especially sympathetic, as even he is unaware of his violent deeds for much of the film; the implication is that these murderous impulses lie dormant until stimulated by trauma or sexual frustration. John Carradine was cast in a similar, if more sadistic role as a murderous painter who kills his models in Edgar G. Ulmer's *Bluebeard*.

These are slightly preceded by two other films that also owe a debt to *M*: producer Val Lewton and director Jacques Tourneur's *The Leopard Man* (1943) and Hitchcock's *Shadow of a Doubt*. Released during a time when the majority of American horror films were campy and escapist, *The Leopard Man* was based on crime writer Cornell Woolrich's grisly novel *Black Alibi*. In the American Southwest, a number of young women are mauled to death and the killings are blamed on an escaped pet leopard. But soon the evidence suggests something more sinister: a human culprit. As in *M*, there is a communal aspect to the film, both in terms of the local reactions to the killings and to the unveiling of the killer himself—also components of *The Lodger* remake and *Hangover Square*.

*Shadow of a Doubt* was allegedly Hitchcock's personal favorite of all his films and marks a turning point in his career. In the 1930s and early '40s, he was primarily focused on espionage films with titles like *The 39 Steps* (1935), *Secret Agent*, *Sabotage* (1936), *The*

*Lady Vanishes* and *Foreign Correspondent* (1940), among others. He also began to explore what could be described as the Gothic woman's film, where a lonely female protagonist finds herself in a threatening environment, often her own domestic space, as in *Jamaica Inn* (1939), *Rebecca* and *Suspicion*. *Shadow of a Doubt* combines this latter trope with the serial killer film, as the protagonist is the teenage Charlie (Teresa Wright), bored by her idyllic life in suburban California. Her beloved namesake, Uncle Charlie (Joseph Cotten), comes to visit, but Charlie learns that her uncle could very well be the Merry Widow Murderer, who seduces and kills wealthy widows.

*Shadow of a Doubt* features a charismatic, sympathetic killer in the form of Joseph Cotten's Uncle Charlie.

Ultimately a film about the loss of innocence and the revelation of the squalid underbelly of the postwar American dream, there is an interesting parallel between Beckert and Uncle Charlie. The latter is sympathetic—as well as charming and handsome—and little explanation is given for his murderous impulses. He defines himself in a series of memorable speeches, including one where we he criticises the 'peaceful, stupid dreams' of Americans and another where he compares his hapless victims to animals lined up for the slaughter. Like Beckert, there is the implication that he's the product of his environment and the notion of a domestic paradise is just a shiny veneer covering a rotten core.

Domestic spaces become monstrous in many films throughout the decade where women are killed, attacked, or psychologically menaced in their homes in far more than just Hitchcock's movies. Lang's fellow emigre from Austria, Otto Preminger, routinely explored this in film noir titles like *Laura* (1944) and *Fallen Angel* (1945), and perhaps the biggest American star of the decade, Humphrey Bogart, was cast as a wife killer in *Conflict* (1945) and *The Two Mrs. Carrolls* (1947), among others. His most important turn as a potential serial killer was in Nicholas Ray's *In a Lonely Place* (1950), a sort-of-descendent of Hitchcock's *The Lodger*. Bogart starred as a troubled, alcoholic writer,

Dixon Steele, who invites a young woman back to his house one night—to explain the plot of a lengthy novel he is supposed to adapt into a script—but he is considered the main suspect when she is later found dead.

His beautiful new neighbour (Gloria Grahame) volunteers an alibi and the two begin a passionate romantic relationship. But Steele becomes paranoid and erratic during the course of the murder investigation and Grahame's character comes to believe that maybe he is the killer after all. Dorothy Hughes's novel of the same name, written in 1947, has a dramatically different approach. In it, Steele is a con artist and murderer, claiming to write mystery novels so that his distant, wealthy family will support him. He has raped and strangled women around the country and in Europe, and killed a wealthy college friend to assume his identity and assets. This latter element was a likely influence on Patricia Highsmith's popular novel, *The Talented Mr. Ripley*, published eight years later. Hughes's intimate, first-person portrayal of a killer also anticipates Jim Thompson's acclaimed crime novel, *The Killer Inside Me*, by five years—all of which, like *M*, feature a killer as the narrative focus.

Ray's film, on the other hand, is less determined to immerse the audience in the psyche of a killer, and more interested in exploring the disintegration of a troubled character who *could* be driven to violence by any number of factors. Like Beckert, a compulsion seems to exist, however buried, within Steele's heart. Steele's life is defined by his bitterness, alienation, alcoholism and lack of control. His self-loathing, paranoia and mistrust of others seeps through the film and it seems inevitable that his innocence would become ambiguous. In the original ending of *In a Lonely Place*, Steele strangles Laurel during their argument. Ray ignored this convenient, if shocking ending. Murder is merely a pretext, a possibility, and Ray's narrative is completely disinterested in who really murdered the coat-check girl, much as *The Lodger* was unconcerned with revealing the real killer.

Murder was often given a motivation like jealousy or greed—a central premise of the majority of film noir titles—and serial killers were still rarely found in these narratives. Lang's friend Robert Siodmak mined this territory for 1945's *The Spiral Staircase*, which combines the earlier themes of a woman suffering from trauma, the home as a place of violence and terror, and a killer stalking vulnerable, young women. One stormy night, a mute girl named Helen (Dorothy McGuire) is in danger when a serial killer begins targeting handicapped women in her neighbourhood and finds his way to the house where she works.

The film focuses on Helen and leaves the identity of the killer a mystery until the conclusion, but presents similar themes of compulsion and mental illness where the killer is concerned. Siodmak, who directed several horror films and thrillers throughout his career, would actually make a film similar to *M* upon his return to Germany in the 1950s: *Nachts, wenn der Teufel kam / The Devil Strikes at Night* (1957), based on the real crimes of Bruno Lüdke, who killed German women in the waning years of WWII. Like *M*, the film speaks to larger issues of social corruption and the failure of justice in the German state.

## LANG'S OTHER SERIAL KILLER THRILLERS

Lang actually also returned to serial killers around the period as well with *Secret Beyond the Door*, itself a reinterpretation of the Gothic woman's film, where a young heiress (Joan Bennett, in her fourth and final collaboration with Lang) meets the dashing, mysterious Mark (Michael Redgrave) on a trip in Mexico. The two quickly marry, but in a re-envisioning of *Bluebeard*, Mark has a number of secrets, including a dead first wife and a room in his forbidding New England mansion that must always stay locked. While Bennett's character is the protagonist of the film, Mark is a sympathetic potential killer, and the film offers up a strangely hopeful—if a touch fantastic—romantic conclusion, when it is revealed that Mark has never acted on his impulses and can perhaps be cured of them by his wife.

Lang's follow up, 1950's *House by the River*, is a far bleaker return to the territory of *M*, with a killer as protagonist. A struggling novelist, Stephen (Louis Hayward) accidentally kills the family's attractive maid (Dorothy Patrick) when she resists his attempts to sexually assault her and then manipulates his troubled brother, John (Lee Bowman), into helping him dump her body in the river. When her body is discovered and a murder trial begins, guilt and mania come between the two brothers. In this film, Lang effectively splits the Beckert character into two: Stephen, a killer possessed by violent sexual compulsions he hides beneath a veneer of civility and domestic normalcy, and John, the eccentric outcast who is openly troubled but has a sort of sympathetic charisma. The film's major structural issue is that it divides running time between the brothers and there is no clear protagonist, but as with *M* and *Secret Beyond the Door*, a sense of lurid sexuality pervades the film.

This is also the case in *While the City Sleeps* and *Beyond a Reasonable Doubt*, where Lang again explores sexually motivated murder. *While the City Sleeps* is an adaptation of Charles Einstein's novel, *The Bloody Spur*, about previously mentioned killer William Heirens, also known as the Lipstick Killer. As in *The Lodger* and *In a Lonely Place*, *While the City Sleeps* puts the murders in the background, focusing mostly on drama in a newsroom investigating and reporting on the crimes. The new owner of a media company (a particularly flowery Vincent Price) declares that whomever identifies the Lipstick Killer will be promoted and this inspires some horrifying competition between the station's division heads. Famed reporter Edward Mobley (Dana Andrews) even mocks the killer live on air and uses his unwitting fiancée as bait to capture a man who breaks into women's homes and strangles them to death.

The frustrated murderer, who is shown on screen, is often paralleled with the men in the newsroom through their callous use of women and the various ways they exploit their own power. In many ways, *While the City Sleeps* picks up where *M* left off and takes a cold, hard look at the media industry—newspapers, television, radio and photography—and presents it as a cynical business driven by men purely interested in profit and sensationalism. The killer is similarly chased through the city at the film's conclusion, bringing to mind larger issues of justice, though it goes further with the psychological themes and prefigures Hitchcock's *Psycho* by attributing psychological trauma and mother issues to its killer, though Lang ultimately asserts that this killer is likely an inevitable product of a predatory, manipulative society.

Lang's final serial killer film, *Beyond a Reasonable Doubt*, which was his last Hollywood film before returning to Germany, is even more subversive. A writer, Tom Garrett (Dana Andrews again), enters into a bargain with his future father-in-law (Sidney Blackmer), an esteemed newspaper publisher, that Tom's next book will be an expose of the corrupt American justice system. They conspire to have Tom framed for the murder of a nightclub dancer, and forge evidence against him. When he is sent to trial, his father-in-law dies, taking the secret to his grave and thus unable to declare Tom's innocence.

His daughter and Tom's fiancée, Susan (Joan Fontaine), is determined to exonerate him. But during her own investigation, she uncovers some surprising evidence that indicates Tom is actually guilty after all. Deeply cynical, *Beyond a Reasonable Doubt* can be read as a critique of McCarthyism, but also of Hollywood's insistence on changing many of Lang's scripts and forcing him to recut his films. It's a film that seems determined to punish its audience and is the culmination of many of *M*'s themes: the killer as sympathetic protagonist, mob justice and media corruption. In a sense, Tom's execution at the end of the film is the act of public exorcism called for by the kangaroo court in *M*, but never realised.

Notably, *M* was remade by director Joseph Losey on its 20-year anniversary, in 1951, under the auspices of the original film's producer, Seymour Nebenzal. Like Lang, Losey's cinema is rife with themes of paranoia, persecution and misguided justice, as he was blacklisted under McCarthyism and forced to relocate to Europe later in the 1950s to continue filmmaking. Losey's *M* fits more comfortably under the moniker of film noir—thanks in part to its Los Angeles setting—and is noticeably a response to the social paranoia and mass hysteria induced by McCarthyism. David Wayne, who stars as child killer Martin Harrow, delivers a much more restrained performance and is even more sympathetic than Beckert, particularly during the mock trial sequences at the end of the film. Initially, Lang's fellow expatriate Douglas Sirk was attached to the remake, but the grisly rewrites he planned for the script were rejected, indicating Hollywood's complicated, though changing attitude about such grim subject matter and on-screen violence. The *M* remake actually foreshadows much of a similar film that would change the face of horror cinema just a few short years later: *Psycho*.

## THE AFTERMATH OF *PSYCHO* AND *PEEPING TOM*

The real watershed moment for modern serial killer films came in 1960, with the release of both Hitchcock's *Psycho* and Michael Powell's *Peeping Tom*. Both of these films operate on the general premise that the central serial killer is a sympathetic figure to be pitied. In general, serial killer films derive their tension from a cat-and-mouse formula, where a detective/victim attempts to uncover the killer's identity, generally at great risk to their own personal safety. This was the predominate model in the 1960s, '70s and '80s in the continuing work of Hitchcock and his descendants, such as American director Brian De Palma, and in cult subgenres like the Italian *giallo* film.

In *giallo* films, for example, a non-professional or amateur detective is pitted against a killer, usually because they have witnessed a vital clue and their testimony (and help in the case) is desired by the police, while they are also pursued by the killer, who is hoping to erase any witnesses. Sometimes, as in Hitchcock's *Rear Window* or a later film like Alejandro Amenábar's *Tesis* (1996), the amateur detective is driven by an inexplicable obsession or compulsion that puts them increasingly in danger, seemingly just to satiate their own curiosity. Another type is the police procedural thriller, such as *Dirty Harry* (1971), where a professional detective hunts down a killer—both because it is their profession and because that is the way law and morality continue to function. In these films, the detective is often changed—morally, but also sometimes psychologically or physically—as a result of this journey.

*Psycho* and *Peeping Tom* deviate from these standard narratives because they follow in the footsteps of *M* and the narrative emphasis is not on a detective or potential victim, but on the killers themselves. *Psycho* arguably lacks a protagonist: in turn, the film follows Marion Crane (Janet Leigh) a woman fleeing with stolen money; her killer, lonely hotel proprietor Norman Bates (Anthony Perkins); and Marion's concerned boyfriend (John Gavin) and her sister (Vera Miles), who have come looking for her. Norman is the most sympathetic figure in the film and, like Beckert, is isolated, even haunted, driven by compulsions he doesn't understand and can't control.

Unlike *M*, Hitchcock doesn't introduce Norman as a killer, though it is apparent that he's disturbed. He explains to Marion that he spends all his time caring for his mentally ill mother and he's an avid taxidermist, particularly fond of the preserving of birds. It's difficult to assess, in a post-*Psycho* world, whether a new viewer coming to the film could possibly be surprised that Norman is Marion's murderer, as his character and the film's plot twist are firmly ingrained in popular culture. Even if this revelation at the end of the film does qualify as a shocking twist, his character type is still similar to Beckert's.

He's not the intelligent, organised and seemingly omniscient killer of later serial killer films. He is lost, lonely and effectively just an abused child trapped in a man's body.

This theme is also a major component of *Psycho*'s competition that year, Michael Powell's *Peeping Tom*. English director Powell made his name with a number of classic films produced in partnership with Hungarian émigré Emeric Pressburger. This later solo film for Powell follows Mark Lewis (Karlheinz Boehm), a photographer and aspiring director, who moonlights as a softcore pornographer and murderer of women. While Norman Bates was the product of a controlling, abusive mother, Mark was raised by a single father; a scientist who frequently used his young son in a series of disturbing psychological experiments about fear. As an adult, he lives in his father's home, which he rents out as a boarding house. Though he develops feelings for a pretty young tenant (Anna Massey), he is unable to control his homicidal urges.

Mark Lewis is unmistakably the protagonist of *Peeping Tom*. He is isolated and lonely, also like Norman Bates, but like Beckert, he is able to disappear into a metropolis: London. Thanks to the city itself—and his various careers—he is surrounded by women who stir his urges, such as prostitutes, dancers and models. Unlike *Psycho*, which became a cultural phenomenon and revolutionised the horror genre, *Peeping Tom* is notorious for nearly destroying Michael Powell's career. Its nihilism, pathos for its killer, and voyeuristic violence horrified audiences and critics alike, though in recent decades it has been re-appraised as a classic. Likely audiences of the day were simply not prepared for the film's lurid themes; pornography features prominently in the plot and the implication is that all types of men want, buy, and look at porn.

While *M* lacks such a simple explanation, both *Psycho* and *Peeping Tom* are reliant upon the concept that psychological trauma is the unspoken motivation for Norman and Mark's violent sexual urges. This would become standard for the majority of serial killer films going forward, particularly those that featured disturbed young men as killer-protagonists. This trend seems to have been building as early as the late '50s with British B-movies like Arthur Crabtree's *Horrors of the Black Museum* (1958), about a writer who runs a museum dedicated to torture, who may view the subject with more than idle curiosity, or Hammer's *The Man Who Could Cheat Death* (1959), about a scientist who murders young women in a search for eternal youth.

While British horror-focused studios like Hammer and Amicus are generally known for their anthology films or adaptations of classic horror literature through *Dracula* and *Frankenstein*, the 1960s and '70s saw an increasing number of thrillers and horror films with a serial killer as protagonist: fairly straightforward thrillers like *Maniac* (1963), *Hysteria* (1965) and *The Psychopath* (1966) gave way to films with complex killer-protagonists like *Night Must Fall* (1964), *The Collector* (1965), *Twisted Nerve* (1968), *I Start Counting* (1969), *Night After Night After Night* (1969), *The Night Digger* (1971), *Hands of the Ripper* (1971), unusual for its female killer, *Straight on Till Morning* (1972) and more.

Many of these films borrowed elements from the so-called British kitchen sink drama, and their protagonists are often angry, isolated and disenfranchised young men from the working classes, lashing out violently against the world. American cinema is stereotypically known for its wealth of serial killer films in the 1970s, '80s and '90s, but these British titles, in tandem with the *giallo*, serve as an example that clearly, by the early 1970s, the serial killer was becoming a mainstay of horror cinema around the world. Several of the films to be released in the 1970s and '80s with serial killer protagonists returned to the example of *M*, in the sense that a lot of them are based on factual killers, such as *The Boston Strangler* (1968) and *10 Rillington Place* (1970), which respectively featured established stars Tony Curtis and Richard Attenborough as their killers.

#### *M*'S CONTINUING LEGACY

While serial killers as a fictional trope have always been associated with the horror genre, thanks to the influence of *M* and the later popularity of *Psycho*, by the 1970s and '80s, serial killer-themed films spread beyond this to arthouse titles and Hollywood blockbusters, a process that has only grown in subsequent decades. Ulli Lommel, an actor and director associated with New German Cinema auteur Rainer Werner Fassbinder, was inspired by *M* for one of his earliest features, *Die Zärtlichkeit der Wölfe / Tenderness of the Wolves* (1973). Produced by Fassbinder, who also has a small role, the film stars regular Fassbinder collaborator Kurt Raab, who also wrote the script, as Weimar-era cannibalistic killer Fritz Haarmann, one of the inspirations for Beckert.

Kurt Raab channels Peter Lorre in *Tenderness of the Wolves*.

Raab intentionally evokes Lorre's performance of Beckert, particularly in his choice of a clean-shaved head and face—in life, Haarmann had short hair, carefully parted, and a moustache. The film plays with the lines between fact and fiction; Raab's Haarmann is soft, passive and emasculated, like Beckert, but this is also likely a reflection of Raab's choice to incorporate homosexual stereotypes—and his own real-life homosexuality— into the role. Like *M*, it incorporates personal trauma with political commentary about Germany's own culpability into its acceptance of fascism. There's even a deliberate homage to Lang with a sequence of a girl playing with a ball, like little Elsie Beckmann.

Serial killer films would only increase in popularity with the emergence of the slasher film in the 1970s and, particularly, '80s, where urban squalour would continue to feature as a prominent factor in the films like *Maniac* (1980) and *Henry: Portrait of a Serial Killer* (1986), both of which have murderers as their focus, or even titles such as William Friedkin's *Cruising* (1980) and Lars von Trier's *Element of Crime* (1984), where an isolated detective protagonist is permanently—and quite nihilistically—transformed in the pursuit of a serial killer. The latest iteration of the subgenre arrived in the '90s with two Hollywood blockbusters: *The Silence of the Lambs* (1991) and *Se7en* (1995).

Based on Thomas Harris's 1988 novel *The Silence of the Lambs*, itself a sequel to 1981's

*Red Dragon*—adapted as *Manhunter* by Michael Mann in 1986—Jonathan Demme's film adaptation has gained a reputation as a masterpiece, both of the horror genre and American cinema in general. Like most of Harris's narratives that involved the refined, cannibalistic serial killer Hannibal Lecter, the film concerns a triangular relationship: between an FBI investigator, Lecter, and a third serial killer still at large. Young FBI trainee Clarice Starling (Jodie Foster) is assigned to interview the imprisoned Dr. Lecter (Anthony Hopkins), a former psychiatrist, to assist in the seemingly unsolvable 'Buffalo Bill' case. Lecter takes a liking to Starling and helps her hunt the mysterious killer who skins women, revealed to be a transsexual named Jame Gumb (Ted Levine).

On the surface, *The Silence of the Lambs* could not be more different from *M*: it follows a detective protagonist and features two serial killers, one of whom is assisting in the capture of the other, if cryptically so. But *The Silence of the Lambs* also pursues themes introduced in *M*, namely the role of voyeurism and surveillance within society itself. Refined, brilliant and seductive, Lecter has become a massively popular cultural phenomenon, with a series of films based on Harris's books and the well-regarded television series, *Hannibal* (2013-2015). Steffen Hantke argues that part of his appeal lies in his ability to transcend conventional structures of power and surveillance:

> In *The Silence of the Lambs*, however, we have a figure that stands for the possibility of a successful escape from surveillance—Hannibal Lecter. Participating in both Starling's and Gumb's spatial iconography, he occupies a middle-ground between those who administer and those who are subject to 'the "word" and the "look"' of institutionalized power.[139]

As in *M*, and the majority of serial killer narratives, these murderers remain all-powerful until they can be seen and named, essentially becoming what Hantke describes as a 'mythical hero', particularly if they are allowed to escape death or punishment and return for sequels:

> They either escape physically, undetected and eager to resume their grisly work, or they transcend their physical limitations and become pure myth. [...] At the same time, these narratives include an endless series of scenes in which the killer himself is ritually murdered, mutilated, or dismembered, his private space invaded and destroyed, and his innermost secrets revealed.[140]

Se7en is yet another reinterpretation of these themes. The film's director, David Fincher, is a contemporary figure upon whom M's influence can be felt quite clearly. He has primarily directed thrillers and horror films throughout his career and returns time and time again to the serial killer narrative. Even his directorial debut, Alien³ (1992), is set on a remote prison planet populated by men with histories of violent crime. But his sophomore effort, Se7en, was to be his breakout hit and seems to borrow key plot elements from M. It follows two detectives (Morgan Freeman and Brad Pitt) on the trail of a killer dubbed John Doe (Kevin Spacey), who is murdering people in New York. His crimes are inspired by the seven deadly sins. As with Fincher's other serial killer film, Zodiac (2007), and his TV series Mindhunter (2017– ), Se7en focuses primarily on its detective protagonists, but subtly borrows from M for its depiction of both the killer and his environment. Se7en depicts the city as hellish, almost post-apocalyptic. Jeremy Tambling writes:

> These corpses and living deaths are discovered in the dull, entropic, fragmented and ruinous atmosphere of a post-industrial city with rain falling perpetually, which recalls both Blade Runner and the rain that falls on the gluttonous in Dante's hell (Inferno 6). The mood of entropy, of the city in decay, finds bodies in decay, beyond death.[141]

Much of the film follows the two detectives as they put together scant clues and pursue the nameless killer throughout the city. Fincher doesn't offer up much sympathy for the victims, who have generally lived lives of excess, sin and squalour. One of the few sympathetic, innocent characters in the film, the younger detective's wife, has doubts about bringing a pregnancy to term in such an environment. She confesses these concerns to the older detective: 'In a private dialogue with Tracy (Gwyneth Paltrow), she tells him of her despair about whether she should have an abortion or not, since she hates the city and the city environment, which is truly paranoia-inducing.'[142]

Tambling notes that another urban-set film with a serial killer as a protagonist, Mary Harron's American Psycho, also references Dante, with graffiti declaring 'Lasciate ogni speranza, voi ch'entrate' ('Abandon all hope, ye who enter here'), a signifier that we are meant to interpret this vision of New York as hell.[143] Similarly, films like Natural Born Killers (1994) and Monster (2003) explore themes of poverty and social issues as the explanation for why the killer protagonists of these films are driven to violence. Fincher would return to this theme in *Panic Room* (2002), when a mother and daughter whose brownstone in New York is infiltrated by criminals, and especially in *Zodiac* (2007), which explores the real-life case of the Zodiac killer, whose Californian killing spree has never been solved. Unlike many other serial killer thrillers, the meditative *Zodiac* focuses on the very anonymity of the killer. Like *M*, this is a source of terror within the film and Fincher explores how the crimes bring together police, media and various other figures in their obsessive attempts to catch a nameless, anonymous killer.

While Fincher would explore serial killers again in his remake of *The Girl with the Dragon Tattoo* (2011) and the potential murder of a woman at the hands of her husband in *Gone Girl* (2014), he has most recently returned to the figure of the sympathetic serial killer with the 2017 television show *Mindhunter*. Following the factual origins of the Behavioral Analysis Unit within the FBI, the show focuses on two agents as they interview incarcerated serial killers and assist baffled local police departments with ongoing investigations. A major figure in the show is Edmund Kemper (Cameron Britton), who has shades of Beckert in his character. Seemingly passive, inept and emasculated, Britton paints the killer as an almost tragic, sympathetic figure who is as much victim as he is villain. *Mindhunter* is a clear example of how the sympathetic serial killer has become an enduring, strangely popular figure since Lang first introduced Beckert with a looming silhouette over a wanted poster and an out-of-tune whistle.

## FOOTNOTES

139. Steffan Hantke, '"The Kingdom of the Unimaginable": The Construction of Social Space and the Fantasy of Privacy in Serial Killer Narratives.' *Literature/Film Quarterly*, Vol. 26, No. 3 (1998), p. 185.
140. Ibid., p. 188.
141. Jeremy Tambling. '"We are Seven": Dante and the Serial Killer.' *Paragraph*, Vol. 22, No. 3 (November 1999), p. 294.
142. Ibid., p. 303.
143. Ibid., p. 294.

# BIBLIOGRAPHY

Allen, Richard J. *Hitchcock's Romantic Irony*. Columbia University Press, 2007.

Brockmann, Stephen. *A Critical History of German Film*. Camden House, 2010.

Butler, Erik. 'Dr. Mabuse: Terror and Deception of the Image.' *The German Quarterly*, Vol. 78, No. 4, Focus on Film (Fall, 2005). pp. 481-495.

Cooke, Anthony Carlton. *Moral Panics, Mental Illness Stigma, and the Deinstitutionalization Movement in American Popular Culture*. Palgrave Macmillan, 2017.

Deutelbaum, Marshall and Leland Poague (eds). *A Hitchcock Reader*. Wiley-Blackwell, 2009.

Eisner, Lotte. *Fritz Lang*. De Capo Press, 1986.

Eisner, Lotte. *The Haunted Screen: Expressionism in the German Cinema and the Influence of Max Reinhardt*. Secker & Warburg, 1973.

Freedman, Estelle B. '"Uncontrolled Desires": The Response to the Sexual Psychopath, 1920-1960.' *The Journal of American History*, Vol. 74, No. 1 (June 1987), pp. 83-106.

Freud, Sigmund. 'The Uncanny.' 1919. http://web.mit.edu/allanmc/www/freud1.pdf

Gay, Peter. *Weimar Culture: The Insider as Outsider*. W. W. Norton & Company, 2001.

Grant, Barry Keith. *Fritz Lang: Interviews*. University Press of Mississippi, 2003.

Gunning, Tom. *The Films of Fritz Lang: Allegories of Vision and Modernity*. British Film Institute, 2000.

Gunning, Tom. '*The Testament of Dr. Mabuse*.' https://www.criterion.com/current/posts/603-the-testament-of-dr-mabuse.

Hantke, Steffen. 'The Kingdom of the Unimaginable': The Construction of Social Space and the Fantasy of Privacy in Serial Killer Narratives.' *Literature/Film Quarterly*, Vol. 26, No. 3 (1998), pp. 178-195.

Hogue, Peter. 'Fritz Lang: Our Contemporary,' *Film Comment*, Vol. 26, No. 6 (November-December 1990), pp. 9-12.

Isenberg, Noah (ed). *Weimar Cinema: An Essential Guide to Classic Films of the Era.* Columbia University Press, 2009.

Jensen, Paul M. *The Cinema of Fritz Lang.* A. S. Barnes & Co., 1969.

Kaes, Anton. 'A Stranger in the House: Fritz Lang's 'Fury' and the Cinema of Exile.' *New German Critique*, No. 89, Film and Exile (Spring - Summer, 2003), pp. 33-58.

Kaes, Anton. *M (BFI Film Classics).* British Film Institute, 2000.

Kaes, Anton. *Shell Shock Cinema: Weimar Culture and the Wounds of War.* Princeton University Press, 2011.

Kemp, Philip. 'The Lodger: A Story of the London Fog: The First True Hitchcock Movie.' https://www.criterion.com/current/posts/4688-the-lodger-a-story-of-the-london-fog-the-first-true-hitchcock-movie.

Kracauer, Siegfried. *From Caligari to Hitler: A Psychological History of the German Film.* Princeton University Press, 2004.

Krajenbrink, Marieke and Kate M. Quinn (eds). *Investigating Identities: Questions of Identity in Contemporary International Crime Fiction.* Rodopi, 2009.

Lang, Fritz. 'My Film *M*: A Factual Report.' https://www.criterion.com/current/posts/1457-my-film-m-a-factual-report.

McElhaney, Joe (ed.). *A Companion to Fritz Lang.* Joe Wiley Blackwell, 2015.

McGilligan, Patrick. *Fritz Lang: The Nature of the Beast.* University of Minnesota Press, 2013.

Nehme, Farran Smith. 'The Man Who Knew Too Much: Wish You Were Here.' https://www.criterion.com/current/posts/2627-the-man-who-knew-too-much-wish-you-were-here

Newton, Michael. *The Encyclopedia of Serial Killers.* Checkmark Books, 2006.

Roth, Joseph. *What I Saw: Reports from Berlin, 1920-1933.* W.W. Norton & Company, 2004.

Shirer, William L. *The Rise and Fall of the Third Reich: A History of Nazi Germany.* Simon & Schuster, 2011.

Smedley, Nick. 'Fritz Lang's Trilogy: The Rise and Fall of a European Social Commentator.' *Film History*, Vol. 5, No. 1 (Mar. 1993), pp. 1-21.

Sova, Dawn B. *Critical Companion to Edgar Allan Poe: A Literary Reference to His Life and Work*. Facts on File, 2001.

Spoto, Donald. *The Dark Side of Genius: The Life of Alfred Hitchcock*. Da Capo Press, 1999.

Stevens, Dana. 'Writing, Scratching, and Politics from M to Mabuse,' *Qui Parle*, Vol. 7, No. 1, Nation and Fantasy (Fall/Winter 1993), pp. 57-80.

Tambling, Jeremy. '"We are Seven": Dante and the Serial Killer.' *Paragraph*, Vol. 22, No. 3 (November 1999), pp. 293-309.

Tatar, Maria. *Lustmord: Sexual Murder in Weimar Germany*. Princeton University Press, 1997.

The Metropolitan Museum of Art. 'Berlin Street.' http://www.metmuseum.org/toah/works-of-art/63.220/.

Thomas, Sarah. *Peter Lorre, Face Maker: Stardom and Performance Between Hollywood and Europe*. Berghahn Books, 2015.

Vronsky, Peter. *Serial Killers: The Method and Madness of Monsters*. Berkley Books, 2004.

Waldron, Dara. *Cinema and Evil: Moral Complexities and the Dangerous Film*. Cambridge Scholars Publishing, 2013.

Youngkin, Stephen D. *The Lost One: A Life of Peter Lorre*. University Press of Kentucky, 2012.

www.ingramcontent.com/pod-product-compliance
Ingram Content Group UK Ltd.
Pitfield, Milton Keynes, MK11 3LW, UK
UKHW022343010326
468527UK00004B/111